Advance Praise

"In Resilient People, Rick Huttner guides us through the pain and shame of his own personal trauma. Every word is real and raw; the reader is forced to viscerally feel the destruction brought on by childhood abuse. He then compassionately leads those who have experienced childhood trauma towards healing and wholeness. Resilient People is a must-read for anyone who has experienced abuse or loves someone who is hindered by the wounds of their past."

—MATTHEW S. STANFORD, PH.D., CHIEF EXECUTIVE OFFICER OF HOPE AND HEALING CENTER & INSTITUTE

"I have known Rick as a friend and past business associate for many years, and also attended personal development workshops with him. I could clearly see his pronounced talents and experienced him as a uniquely charming, intelligent, and generous person. Yet, as he so adeptly reveals, something was awry. His willingness to 'go the distance' to root out the extremely debilitating emotional damage, pain, and suffering caused by childhood sexual abuse is courageous in itself. To openly share in the detail that he has in Resilient People, and to provide a clear guide to healing for those having had similar experiences, is nothing short of remarkable!"

—ROBERT BEALE, PRESIDENT OF BEALE INTERNATIONAL, AUTHOR OF *THE GOLDEN PATH TO ONENESS* AND *EXPERIENCING ONENESS*

"This book is informative, honest, real, and relevant. The pages take you on a powerful journey that honors and acknowledges the broken experience of the abused and discusses how to put the pieces back together again. It turns up the volume as a voice to be heard throughout society regarding the pain and confusion which abuse instills in victims. It also shines a light on the ways to find resilience, freedom from the past, and a heart-opening return to life as it was meant to be lived. This is a book of hurt, healing, and a return to happiness."

—HOWARD CAESAR, SENIOR MINISTER (RETIRED) AT UNITY CHURCH OF CHRISTIANITY, AUTHOR OF *ONE + ONE = ONE*

Resilient People

Resilient People

A Journey from Childhood Abuse
to Healing & Love

Rick Huttner

COPYRIGHT © 2019 RICK HUTTNER
All rights reserved.

RESILIENT PEOPLE
A Journey from Childhood Abuse to Healing and Love

ISBN   978-1-5445-0309-7 *Paperback*
        978-1-5445-0310-3 *Ebook*

Dedicated to the millions of abused children:

Know that you did nothing wrong and that you can heal.

Contents

Foreword 11
Introduction 13

PART I: THE EFFECTS OF ABUSE
1. My Story Begins 27
2. The Psychology and Facts of Child Abuse 51
3. My Story Continues: Healing 85

PART II: THE HEALING TRAJECTORY
4. Becoming Aware of the Signs of Abuse 109
5. My Story Continues: Waking Up to
   Self-Defeating Patterns 139
6. Finding a Safe Place to Talk and Share 159
7. Locating a Professional Therapist
   Trained to Treat Abuse Survivors 175
8. Fighting the Cycle of Child Abuse 191

Conclusion 215
Appendix 223
Acknowledgments 227
About Frederick "Rick" Huttner 231

Foreword

People grow emotionally as trees do physically, from the inside out. The tender germinated sprout is there inside the tallest oak. Within the human, this fragile self is the inner child, who experiences every interaction as a key to self-worth. Wound the child and the mark may be scarred over, buried, worked around, and compensated for—but not healed. What is hidden will eventually display itself, perhaps in tormented dreams or patterns of self-sabotage and emotional absence. The exiled self will come up for healing. For this, the individual and all of society must be prepared.

As Rick Huttner reminds us again and again in this book, children are not to blame for what happens to them. His words are so powerful because he is principally telling *himself* this, while permitting us to witness his years-long painful resurrection into effective and compassionate manhood.

Many works on the subject of child abuse are therapist-authored, with italicized case notes from anonymous clients. All help somebody, sometime. But nothing I've read comes within a mile of the searing, unsparing story Rick recounts of his journey back from the edge of oblivion. Had it just ended with a new dawn for Rick and as a cautionary tale for everyone else, this book would have been enormously courageous and done much good. But Rick's inclusion of data, notes, resources, and guidelines for selecting the right counselor and venue for support carries the healing mission from his life into ours.

Rick's message is essential for abuse survivors, for all who care about them, for anyone who wants to nurture children, and for those of us who aren't willing to wait for subsequent generations to be born and die off before society learns to cherish and safeguard its children.

Well done, Rick—and *bravo, Freddy.*

JESSE JENNINGS, DOCTOR OF DIVINITY
SENIOR MINISTER OF CREATIVE LIFE CENTER,
COLUMNIST FOR *SCIENCE OF MIND* MAGAZINE
MARCH 12, 2019

Introduction

The room was dark—very dark. In the middle of it was a small child, sitting alone. Terror filled the child's mind. He knew that someone was coming, someone who wanted to hurt him. The fear mounted. I could see the child's face, mouth open wide, contorted with trying to scream, but unable to make a sound. The sounds from the person approaching got louder. I could see the child try to raise a gun and point it at the door. No matter how hard he tried, he couldn't pull the trigger. He was helpless: helpless to stop the terror; helpless to stop the pain.

I would wake up soaked in sweat and terrified.

The night terrors came once or twice a week, for close to fourteen years. I had become an expert in burying the pain while I was awake, making "friends" out of alcohol, distractions, and risk-taking. They all helped deaden the pain—but the pain found its way out while I slept.

I've spent a lifetime making that pain go away.

THE PREVALENCE OF ABUSE

I was abused as a kid, like countless others. In the United States, approximately 7.4 million children are abused every year, either psychologically, physically, or sexually—and that figure is probably underreported.[1] Abuse isn't something people like to talk about, especially the abusers. A beaten child is taken to the emergency room covered in bruises, but the nurses are told, "She fell down the stairs." What should be reported as a criminal offense gets covered up, protecting the perpetrator and keeping the victim in a cycle of abuse.

Why doesn't the abused person speak up? In my experience, it's because there's incredible confusion about who is to blame. Most abusers endear themselves to the children they target before abuse starts, and the children start out genuinely loving those people. As abuse begins and continues, the "trusted" perpetrators tell lies about the harm they're inflicting: "This is special. This is love. You made me do it. I couldn't help myself." Typ-

---

[1] "Child Abuse Statistics," American SPCC, accessed December 6, 2018, https://americanspcc.org/child-abuse-statistics/.

ically, victims of abuse wind up blaming themselves. In my case, I believed I had committed an unforgivable sin. Perpetrators are amazingly skilled at putting guilt on the people they're hurting. So the abused make excuses for the abusers—and the cycle continues.

Despite the countless instances of abuse in our world, people still don't want to talk about it. The #MeToo movement is a wonderful example of women saying "Enough" and bringing instances of abuse into the light. However, it says something about our culture that it's taken this long for us to have a reckoning. Think about all the abuse that was brought to light in this movement—all the abuse that had been hidden for decades. Think of all the women who tried to speak up but were initially shut down or not believed. Think of all that it took for the movement to finally happen.

Now think about the countless acts of abuse inflicted on children. Do they have a voice? Can they coordinate, the way these adult women have, to find strength in numbers? Can they network to combine their testimonies and bring down their abusers? No. Abused children are told not to speak about abuse; they are often threatened to keep quiet or face harsh consequences.

Children are our most vulnerable members of society, and they have no voice to fight abuse. Like the child in my nightmare, they try to open their mouths, but nothing comes out. They need someone to speak up on their behalf, and that's one of the goals of this book. It's our job to advocate for them, to give them a voice, to show them how to be healed.

REPRESSED TRUTH

Abuse is tough to talk about—and no one knows that better than I do. For years, I avoided feeling anything. It felt safer to be numb than to deal with what happened. But still, the events that happened were determined to deal with me. The night terrors were a message that something had happened. Although I couldn't pinpoint what it was at the time—so deeply had I buried these painful memories—the dreams stirred up profound terror and pointed to *something*.

Denial is a powerful coping mechanism among survivors of abuse. It's too painful to face the fact that abuse happened, so it gets buried or denied. We tell ourselves that physical and sexual abuse was somehow our fault or that verbal abuse must have somehow been warranted.

None of that is true. It was not your fault. This is vital for you to know. I'd like to yell this message out from the pages of this book: it was not your fault!

You may have a list of excuses in your mind to downplay

a harmful experience that was inflicted on you. You may recognize a series of destructive patterns in your life and write them off as your own bad choices. You may experience a daily fight with negative emotions and ignore their possible source. But hear the message your subconscious may be shouting at you: *if you feel you might have been abused, chances are you were.*

Even if abuse was not long-lasting or violent, it can still cause long-term damage, particularly in children. I remember hearing about a woman who was abused by her father. When she started developing breasts as a girl, her father would put his hand down her blouse and squeeze her nipples. He thought this was funny, but it terrified her. As an adult, she hated her breasts. Even in loving romantic relationships, the woman would experience shock waves of trauma when a man touched her chest. As Laura Davis wrote in *Allies in Healing*, "The most important thing in defining child sexual abuse is the experience of the child. It takes very little for a child's world to be devastated."[2]

If you suspect you may have experienced abuse, it's important to explore your feelings about that in a proper setting. I was fortunate enough to eventually find a safe, therapeutic environment in which to finally face some of

---

[2] Laura Davies, *Allies in Healing* (New York: Harper Collins, 1993).

my past trauma. I believe that, as long as abuse remains repressed, survivors will be plagued by damaging effects.

THE EFFECTS OF ABUSE IN LATER LIFE

Abuse can come in many forms: psychological, physical, sexual, neglect, or some horrible combination. The effects of abuse are even more varied. Roughly a third of abused children grow up to abuse their own children, continuing a cycle of abuse. Abuse survivors are more likely to have unprotected sex and commit crimes.[3] There's a long list of emotional, psychological, and neurological effects that are caused by abuse as well.

The shame and fear that typically affect abuse survivors show up in any number of ways. For instance, my given name is Frederick, and I'd always gone by "Freddy" as a child. In the aftermath of abuse, I developed a stutter and could no longer introduce myself as "Freddy"; I ended up switching my name to "Rick." I wet the bed for years. I was afraid of other boys. If a fight threatened to break out, I was paralyzed; I couldn't defend myself.

Even when a child grows up and seems to be doing well, a self-destructive streak may follow them. I became a successful businessman, but I made a series of bad deci-

---

[3] "Child Abuse Statistics," American SPCC, accessed December 6, 2018, https://americanspcc.org/child-abuse-statistics/.

sions throughout my career that I believe were driven by a buried sense of shame. When something good came along—whether that was a beautiful relationship or professional success—deep within me, I would think, *I don't deserve this.* Then I'd ruin it.

Particularly if abuse occurs during childhood, a child's brain gets rewired. We begin to "think wrong," and that leads to a lot of bad decisions down the road. Survivors of abuse experience shame, along with a profound sense of worthlessness. They believe if they had real value, the abuse would have never occurred. Since it did occur, their feeling of worthlessness is confirmed.

Some survivors of abuse self-mutilate, believing that they need punishment for doing something wrong. Some people ruin their marriages with affairs or deviant sexual behavior. They're unable to experience true satisfaction in an intimate relationship because of scars in their past, so they pursue satisfaction elsewhere, only to encounter the same problems. Some people self-medicate, trying to cover the pain with drugs and alcohol; alternately, they might experience bouts of rage when the pain explodes. In the most tragic cases, people commit suicide.

We have what I call demons. These demons of fear burrow deep into our subconscious mind. The more we push them down, the more powerful they become. They come back to haunt us, exploding out in moments of intense emotion. They'll continue to gain power over us until we decide it's time to confront them.

HEALING IS POSSIBLE

Pain, shame, worthlessness—those are not the end of the story. We are incredibly resilient people. Inside all of us is a spark that will help lead us towards healing, if we listen to it. I believe that when a decision is made to heal, the Universe will help you towards that end in ways you could not imagine.

But that healing isn't going to come from something outside of us. I can't tell you how many healing seminars I went to. I got bodywork, massage, Reiki—but none of that worked. I kept looking to be healed, not to heal. Finally, I started examining some of the hard issues of my past, looking at the patterns of abuse and my patterns of self-destruction. Once I began to look inside, true healing began.

The first step towards healing is to explore what happened to you. It's terrifying to go there. I spent my life looking for ways to avoid self-examination. Demons are repressed fears; they've been driven deep into the subconscious mind. Although deep, they can leak out. They can easily trigger negative responses, which prevent us from being open. Rather than be vulnerable, we turn to rage, apathy, pride, or self-medication, and those demons grow more powerful. But I know the demons can dissipate when they're put into the light.

When I finally began to shine the light on my inner darkness and confront the trauma in my past, the healing it produced was invigorating. It was so energizing, in fact, that for a while, I couldn't shut up about it. I'd be in a social setting with friends having a casual conversation, and I'd start opening up about my past and weep. My wife experienced a lot of awkward moments with me as her social companion!

Eventually, I found the right places to do it: safe places, with people who were trained in counseling abuse survivors. I learned what a potent tool writing could be, which enabled me to more deliberately choose my thoughts. The mind is powerful. By paying attention to my thoughts, I could take control of my mind and heal myself of negative beliefs.

There's no one formula to help a person heal from abuse; every survivor must take his or her own journey. However, there are some important common denominators, and that's what I want to share in this book.

WHO I AM

I'm Frederick Huttner, once known as Freddy, now known as Rick. I suffered both physical and sexual abuse when I was a child, and the effects plagued me for years. But I healed. My healing came late in life, but I actually did heal. I'm a testament to the fact that healing can happen, and it's never too late. After years of pain and brokenness, I can now honestly say that I'm having a wonderful time. I love my wife, and we have a beautiful and caring relationship. I run a consulting practice, which enables me to help other people. My kids love me. I'm free from the demons of my past, and I'm able to look for the good in life.

I could have started experiencing this freedom thirty years ago. It's my hope that, with this book, I can help other people find healing sooner rather than later. I want other survivors of abuse to know *they did nothing wrong, and they can heal.*

The Resilient People Initiative was founded with this objective in mind: We deliver talks that let abuse survivors know they're not alone. We provide resources to help people find ways to begin their own healing process. We remind people of their true inner resilience and share the healing trajectory that I and many others have experienced.

This book can be part of that healing process.

Resilience is rooted deep in the mind and spirit. It's the inner voice that reminds us we were born perfect; we are children of the Divine. Although many of us have been harmed and carry inner demons, there is a powerful spark within each one of us. When that spark of resilience gets lit, light floods in, and we can start the journey back towards freedom and healing.

Will you take that journey with me?

Part I

The Effects of Abuse

CHAPTER ONE

My Story Begins

Abuse and Its Aftermath

My mother was overwhelmed. That doesn't excuse it, but it helps explain it.

I was her fourth child, born just thirteen months after my next-oldest brother—most likely an unanticipated addition. During a family vacation in the Catskills, which she must have been looking forward to, news came that shook her to the core. A state policeman knocked on the door and asked, "Are you Mrs. Huttner?" When she replied yes, he said simply, "Your mother died." Then he walked away.

She was traumatized. I think her life was connected to her mother, and especially so while she was struggling as a mother herself, trying to raise four sons. There was no support to be found from her father—if anything, he added to her stress. I remember him once looking at our house and saying, "I think I'm going to tear this down." He scared the bejesus out of me. Grandfather later wound up in Orangeburg State Hospital, essentially a mental institution. My mother made us go visit him. The doors locked behind us, and we all had to go in and kiss Grandpa. I didn't want to put my face near him. I just wanted to get out of there.

Something happened in our family shortly after my grandmother's death—something bad, something that my family never talked about.

A clue about this period came when my older brother put all of our family photos in order. My family is of German extraction, with a long tradition of costume parties. There were loads of pictures of my parents with their friends at different people's houses, all in various getups. Right after the end of 1945, it stopped. There are a few pictures after that, but nothing of the partying or the family—nothing of the smiles.

Another clue came years later, when I was chatting with relatives. My aunt mentioned a memory from when I lived with her as a young child. I had no idea that I'd ever lived with relatives, but I later found out that my brothers and I had all been placed with various extended family members during a span of time following my grandmother's death.

As it turns out, during this period, my mother had been sent away.

I believe she was sent away because she'd tried to kill me.

PHYSICALLY ABUSED

For the next several decades, I was haunted by this trauma, although as a child, I understood nothing about what had actually happened. I was only a baby when my grandmother died, so I don't remember anything about that time. I was only able to collect fragmented details as an adult.

What I pieced together is this: when I was six months old, my mother had a serious nervous breakdown. The trauma of losing her mother, along with the dysfunction in her birth family and the added stress of raising us kids was too much. All of Mother's pent-up grief and anger came out in violence against me. She was sent away—I don't know where or for how long. My three brothers and I were separated and sent to live with different relatives.

No one ever talked about why this all happened, and no

one in my family has wanted to answer my questions for more information.

My mother never fully admitted what she tried to do to me. The closest she ever came to telling me was late in her life when I visited her in Florida. She couldn't specifically say what she'd done, but acknowledged that *something* had happened. She only said, "I was so afraid I would hurt you, I had to send you away."

I've wondered: were her feelings of anger so intense towards me as an infant that I interpreted her actions in my dreams as attempted murder? As I've worked through anger and forgiveness in my later years, maybe I'm trying to soften it for myself. I don't know. My dreams told a different story. They were so incredibly vivid, I don't know how I could have created them.

As a result of what happened, I believe Mother was driven by guilt. She became very involved in our Lutheran church, participating in the choir, serving on the board, doing special projects—everything. Although I suspect she was doing this in part to "atone" for trying to hurt me, her church membership ended up straining our relationship even more. She got so involved with the church, she spent little time with her youngest son. As far as I was concerned, in committing her life to God, she left me out.

Mother forced us to participate as well. We had to go to church—the early service, no less. I grew to hate it. In my opinion, our minister was the most boring speaker in the world. Every time I thought he was coming to the end of his sermon, his train of thought would die off and he'd start up again on a new point. My father used to mutter, "We've got to get out of here." I could go to a Lutheran service and recite every prayer and sing every hymn, but all the while, I'd be thinking about my high school sweetheart. That was more fun than doing the liturgy.

I equated religion with my mother, and I didn't trust my mother at all. She had only ever made me feel like an unwanted event. In my mind, it was religion that caused me to be alone and unloved. I hated it.

REPRESSED MEMORIES MAKING THEMSELVES KNOWN

I was too young to "remember" my mother's attack, but the trauma from the event followed me for many years. Abused children experience all kinds of effects from maltreatment, and I was no exception. I wet my bed for far too long. Around the same time, I started having the night terrors. There were two recurring dreams.

In my first dream, I had a feeling like I was in a constricted space, like a crib. Everything was gray and blurry. I felt pressure on my throat and my neck, and I knew I was going to be hurt. I *knew* it. There was a sureness and a horror that someone was going to hurt me. I tried to fight the pressure on my throat, but the more I fought it, the worse the pressure got. I couldn't scream or make a sound, but I'd fight to scream and cry until I couldn't fight anymore. The dream only ended after I surrendered to the terror and gave up. I'd wake up soaked in sweat and terrified—breathing crazily and consumed with total abject fear.

In the second dream, I was in that same room. It was dark again, and still gray. I was little but I held a handgun. I heard someone coming. I knew they were going to hurt me—maybe even kill me. I raised the gun at the person approaching, but I couldn't pull the trigger, no matter how hard I tried. I could see my face contorted, my mouth open to scream—but I could never make a sound.

And again, I'd wake up dripping with sweat, feeling scared out of my mind.

The dreams came at least once a week. I had them until I was about twenty-eight. Maybe I should have figured out that such terrifying recurring nightmares were connected to trauma, but at that point in my life, I wasn't interested in exploring pain. My tendency was the exact opposite: I explored numbing agents, and my agent of choice was alcohol.

In my late twenties, I had three close friends all confront me about my drinking. Their combined urging, along with the fact that I was jeopardizing my job if I didn't get help, caused me to enter into therapy for the first time.

SEEKING HELP

I started off in individual therapy with a wonderful couple. Eventually, I moved into a group. The group became a place where I felt safe and cared for. I was treated like there was nothing wrong with me. Sure, I had some issues, but they were just "issues." The issues weren't *me*—they were something to work through and move on from. That was a big shift from how I'd been treated (and how I'd treated myself) for most of my life.

During one session, I was sharing about the night terrors. Unconsciously, I was rubbing my left arm with my right hand—I used to do that a lot. My counselor brought that up. "Rick," he said, "what's up with your left arm?" He paused, then added, "Have you ever noticed that you're always rubbing somebody's back in here and trying to take care of people? You're giving away what you want and need. You're trying to love yourself." His words hit on truth, and I started to feel powerful emotions stir up in me.

Other people in the group started speaking up, and my counselor said, "Everybody stop." He moved right in front of me. "Rick. Tell me what you're doing, rubbing your left arm." I started getting agitated—his question struck something deep, and I didn't totally understand what. Then he asked, "Who abused you?"

I felt my heart go cold. I started crying uncontrollably at the realization that I was abused. They put me in a rage position, which is not a violent hold—you're held and braced so you don't hurt yourself or anyone else. All the tears and anger flowed out of me. The group held me, letting me scream and yell and cry. I don't know how long it lasted. I was physically exhausted for a long time afterwards. But the experience was an unbelievable relief. It was like a dam breaking. I just cried and cried.

When it finally ended, I said, "*I know.* I know what the dreams mean—I know what happened to me." The group had heard about the recurring nightmares, but I'd never been able to pinpoint a source for them. Somehow, the release of that moment enabled repressed memories to come to the surface. I realized I was *little*. I couldn't stop my mother from hurting me. I couldn't defend myself.

After I had that realization, I never had one of those dreams again. The fact that they stopped immediately confirmed to me that I'd hit on the truth. Releasing all that rage felt like a lifetime of pain flowing out of me—but in fact, I was only beginning my deep healing. This was just the tip of the iceberg.

SEXUALLY ABUSED

My parents used to take my brothers and me to the Catskills when we were kids. They'd bought an old one-room schoolhouse in a beautiful valley in rural New York. My father dropped the ceiling to create a bedroom upstairs; you couldn't stand up straight under the slope of the roof. We all slept up there, parents and kids. There was no phone, no radio, no TV. We used a wood stove for heating, gathering the wood from the forest around us.

The early summers were idyllic. We built tree houses and climbed the poplar trees, getting as high as we could until our weight forced the trees to bend and drop us to the ground, then snapping back up. We had three swimming holes. Otter Falls was our secret; the river came down and carved its way through the rock, creating a smooth shoot, like a waterslide. We'd drop into the river, and it would take us through a number of turns, then drop us into a big pool of freezing mountain water. It was beautiful. Crazy Nelsons was a waterfall that came down about thirty feet into a small pool. At Parker Falls, the upper falls poured into a solid rock basin that you could walk through, then it came down another shoot into what we called the "fat man's bathtub." On the other side of that was Parker Falls, which we would dive off. As a kid, it felt like an eternity going down, but it was probably only twenty-five feet. We played badminton and hiked and climbed mountains—it was a wonderful place to grow up.

My family had a friend, Bob, who was the local policeman. It was a small town, so everyone knew Bob, and we all liked him. Bob stopped by our house often. One day, during the summer that I was twelve, he asked my parents if he could take me for a ride in his police car. I was ecstatic when they said yes—what a thrill! He turned the lights on and pulled people over while I was still in the car. I was in heaven! He also bought me my first gun, a Mossberg .22, and taught me how to care for it.

Bob gave me the attention I'd always craved, especially from my father. Dad was a German immigrant who constantly worked to make a better life for his family. He was a good man, and a loving man, but he didn't know how to goof off with his sons. Bob, on the other hand, tagged along with us when we went swimming and played games with us. I loved the guy.

The following summer, when I was thirteen, I was excited

to hang out with Bob again. He was around more and more. He'd often take my friends and me swimming at our favorite spots and took me on special outings. One day after we finished swimming, he said, "Freddy, I've got to go back to my house to pick something up. Then I'll run you home." That sounded fine to me; I didn't think anything of it.

When we got to his apartment, he said, "Come on up. I've got to put some stuff together." I followed him up the stairs and into his place, still not questioning anything. Then Bob said, "I'm tired, Freddy. I'm going to lie down." He lay on his bed and looked over at me. "Come join me," he suggested.

Bob was my friend, and I trusted him. I followed his instructions and lay down beside him. As I was laying there, Bob put his hand on my stomach. My body tensed up—something didn't feel right. Slowly, he put his hand down into my swim trunks and started massaging my penis.

My mind began sending off alarms—I was confused and scared. Panic started taking over me, but I didn't know what to do. Then I looked over at Bob, and he'd gotten his penis out. He was rubbing it up and down, masturbating.

I couldn't understand what was happening. I knew

nothing about sex. My parents had never talked to me about any of that, and I hadn't even hit puberty yet. In 1958, there was no internet or social media to tip me off about the "birds and the bees"; the cabin didn't even have a radio or a television. I was totally innocent about sexual issues.

In the midst of my confusion, my body convulsed, and I had an orgasm. The experience was terrifying. I'd never had an erection; I'd never had wet dreams; I'd never even *heard* of an orgasm. Afterwards, Bob said, "Freddy. This is so beautiful between us. This is so incredibly special. I love you so much, Freddy. You can *never, ever* talk to anybody about this."

Bob was a cop. He arrested people and carried a gun. He was friends with my parents. And he swore me to secrecy because—he said—he loved me so much. But I've since realized that Bob's command created the basis for shame: he demanded secrecy and silence. As a result, I carried judgment. For twenty years, I obeyed him. I never told a soul.

Bob abused me like this a number of times. Then came the pornographic movies and magazines he'd show me. The movies were degrading; none of them would teach a young boy how to have tender, loving sex with a woman. Another day, he took me to his neighbor's house, and I was alone with two men. They put on a reel-to-reel porn tape, and we started watching it. I don't remember what happened after that. I know I was abused. But my conscious mind has stayed black about the details.

At the end of the summer, I overheard adults talking at the Valley View Boarding House; they didn't know I was around. The adults were talking about Bob, and one of them commented, "Yeah, he really likes young boys." They all laughed. I started thinking, *something is really wrong here*. But I couldn't pin the blame on Bob. Like many abused children, I couldn't understand that such a trusted adult was actually in the wrong.

I concluded that this had to be my fault. I had done something terribly, terribly wrong. I'd committed some unforgivable sin. I didn't understand it was the responsibility of the caregiver to look after the child. I didn't know that—and so I carried that shame for a long, long time.

COPING MECHANISMS, ISOLATION, AND FEAR

Life fell apart when we went back home after the summer. I developed a stutter so severe I couldn't introduce myself; "Freddy" was almost impossible for me to pronounce. I couldn't answer questions. I remember moments in school when the teachers would have us take turns reading. I never heard what anybody said, because

I was figuring out if I'd be able to pronounce what I had to read. Most often, I knew I couldn't.

At age fourteen, I started sneaking alcohol. I didn't want to feel. The memories of abuse terrified me; I felt huge guilt and shame anytime I thought about it. By the time I was sixteen, I found out I could pass for eighteen in the bars, which was the legal drinking age in New York. It became easier to drink, so I drank more. I had to deaden the painful feelings. When I couldn't get alcohol and I had to find another way to keep the fear down, I masturbated to calm myself. That became another compulsive coping mechanism.

I got into petty theft as well. I remember one Christmas, my buddies and I grabbed lights off houses and smashed them. That year, I stole to get all the gifts I gave people—gloves, pens, everything. When my family opened the gifts, no one asked me where I'd gotten the money to buy them. I think I was hoping they would. I knew my actions were a cry for help, but my family didn't talk to each other. There were no questions asked.

People called me a "hood." I didn't have many close friends, and I wasn't close with my brothers. I was an introvert and spent much of my time alone. Still, girls liked "the bad boy." I could always get a girl—but whenever the relationship got close to real intimacy, it fell apart.

I remember dating a girl from my church when I was sixteen. One day we were over at my friend's house while his mother was out of town. My girlfriend and I went into his mother's bedroom and started heavy petting. I wanted to touch her more than anything, but I was afraid. I had no idea how to treat a woman. The experience scared me and shamed me. I ended my relationship with her soon afterwards.

Because of my stutter, my teachers assumed I was a slow learner and put me in a vocational school. After high school, I worked menial jobs. I was a driver's helper on a UPS truck; I worked in a print shop. I worked at the World's Fair as a rent-a-cop, then I got a job at a metal factory. Eventually, I ended up in Vietnam.

Ironically, I felt safe in Vietnam. In spite of being in a chaotic jungle, everything about my experience felt controlled. I knew when I had to get up; I knew when I had to eat; I knew when it was time for lights out. Something about the predictability felt reassuring. Still, it was lonely. When you think of war, you think of *Band of Brothers*, but my position within my battalion kept me isolated. I had more privileges than a lot of officers, which meant many of them didn't like me. Nothing about being in the military helped me connect with other men; it just made me feel more alone. After thirteen months, I was abruptly sent home. Two weeks later, I was back home and a social pariah. Nobody liked the Vietnam veterans. I couldn't be proud about having served my country.

Then, a beautiful young lady came into my life. I remember I was standing on a corner waiting for a bus, to go to work. A girl I knew from church drove by. She rolled the window down and smiled big at me. We started dating. Once again, though, just like with my previous sweetheart, I couldn't handle the intimacy. We dated for a long time and eventually got engaged. One afternoon, we got close to making love, and I got terrified all over again. Shortly after that, I started breaking it off. One day, I called her up and said, "I want my ring back." I drove over to her house, got it, ignored the pictures she offered me of our time together, and then drove away. I was cold.

In some sick way, that kept me safe. I didn't have to deal with feelings. I'd spent so much of my life deadening the painful feelings that I didn't know how to have *any* strong feeling—even love. I'd deadened them all. I treated these two ladies terribly, but I didn't know how to treat a woman any differently. My sexual development had been hijacked—it had been totally inappropriately diverted. The "education" I'd gotten about sex from the pornographic movies I'd been shown involved being cruel or degrading to woman. I didn't want to do that to either of these ladies—so I just ran.

SUBSTANCE ABUSE AND SELF-SABOTAGE

After Vietnam, I used the GI Bill to go back to school, eventually enrolling in NYU. That was another lonely season for me; there was a prominent anti-war group on campus, and NYU is a liberal school. Vets were generally shunned; I had no social life.

After graduation, I moved to upstate New York and went to work for a builder on a ski center. My boss was abusive as hell; he fit right into my pattern of attracting abusive people. I found another job, but once again landed in a toxic situation. My boss and coworkers got high and partied together, so I began to add drugs to my self-medicating routine.

Around the same time, I reconnected with a childhood friend, Bernie, who was now a state trooper. Bernie and I did insane things. I remember "threading the needle," racing through tollbooths at crazy speeds. I got into multiple motorcycle accidents, one after I'd taken a quaalude. I didn't even ask what it was—I just took it. After I got high, I approached an intersection where cars were stopped. I downshifted, then accelerated—I thought I was going to fly over all the cars in front of me. I *did* fly, as a matter of fact. My motorcycle rammed into the rear of the car and launched my body over the vehicles in front of me. I wound up in the middle of the intersection and was hauled away to the hospital. The fact that I didn't kill myself or anyone else still amazes me.

Finally, I determined I had to get away from the drugs. My solution was to get a job at a bar. The job was good for me; I didn't drink while I was tending bar, and I enjoyed the interaction with people. I loved the fact that there was a thick counter between us: none of the conversation was intimate. I was good at remembering drink orders, and I loved joking around with people. It was safe. I didn't develop relationships—except, that is, when I met my future wife.

This attractive lady came in one day, and she wanted Irish coffee. We didn't have it, so she said, "See you next week," and left. I went out and made sure we got Irish whiskey. The woman showed up again a week later, and I served her an Irish coffee. She thought that was wonderful. I was the best guy in the world! We decided to date, and eventually, I asked her to marry me.

We were crazy about each other—and we were a mess. She'd had a difficult childhood and came from a dysfunctional family. Neither of her parents were thrilled about our relationship, and marrying me, I think, was her way of rebelling.

We truly loved each other when we got married, but as the old saying goes, when we moved in together, we brought so much baggage, there wasn't room for both of us. She had abuse issues. I struggled with anger and had abuse issues as well, which I hadn't even begun to explore at that time. We tried therapy repeatedly and unsuccessfully.

My drinking began to escalate. Right after getting married, my wife and I moved from New York to Florida, where I joined a CPA firm. It was socially acceptable at that time to go out and have a martini at lunch, so I'd help myself to one or two. When I got home from work, I'd drink some more.

Once, when my wife's parents were in town, we hosted a volleyball party with a bunch of friends. I drank my first beer in the morning, which I thought was cool. By the afternoon, I was hammered. My brother-in-law was trying to take his motorcycle up a steep hill, and I grabbed the bike from him. It was the stupidest thing in the world to get on a motorcycle when I was so intoxicated, but I roared up the mountain and lost control. The bike flipped over and landed on top of me; I hit the ground flat on my back. It hurt like hell. Even through the haze of pain and drunkenness, I could see how people were looking at me. *Holy shit*, their faces said. *This guy is out of control.*

And I was. I was out of control. I didn't know how to heal my marriage and knew even less about how to heal myself. I had no idea how to be vulnerable. My wife and I would try to talk through these tough issues in therapy, but she ran from them, and I numbed them away. I had no emotional capability to go within. We finally divorced after about four years.

One truly beautiful thing came out of that relationship: my daughter, Mesia. She's the best gift of my life. I was involved with my wife's pregnancy and was present for the entire labor process. I was even allowed to deliver Mesia! When that little life came into my hands, something deep inside of me was profoundly moved. It awoke a love in me I had not been aware of, nor ever known. I looked down at this precious child, my baby girl, and thought how desperately I wanted her to have a good life. Mesia and I are still close. I love her deeply.

The self-destructive tendencies that contributed to that divorce affected my career too. I kept screwing things up. At the CPA firm, I didn't know how to reconcile something on a bank job, so I made up an answer. When my boss called me on it, I quit. Then I went to work for a small construction firm. When we had the annual audit, part of me got scared, so I faked the flu. I didn't help the auditor at all. I ended up getting demoted and thought, *The hell with this*. I got out my résumé again.

I did well at the next job initially, but then still found a way to tank it. I worked as an accountant for a paper firm, which was an amazing mess: it made a ton of money and wasted almost as much. I spent months cleaning it all up. By the end of a lot of late nights and weekends at the office, the place was a smooth-running machine.

So what did I do? I celebrated with a drink. Or rather, *drinks*. I began taking longer and longer lunches, usually coming back less than sober. Finally, my assistant and my boss confronted me. My boss gave me an ultimatum: get help or get a new job. That's when I started therapy and made the discovery about my mother's abuse. Even in counseling, though, the unhealthy habits followed me. I made an agreement with my counselor to only have one beer a day—so I'd find the biggest beer I possibly could. I remember him shaking his head when he figured that out: "Sneaky."

I can't count how many times I sabotaged myself. I'd get involved with a business, increase its profit by millions, and then find a way to lose it. Other times, I would be doing great things for a company, but I'd allow someone else in the business to make a decision that I knew would tank it. I was drawn to charismatic, abusive personalities. In one situation, I'd been given clear reasons to distrust someone, but I did another deal with him anyway—one which landed me in a four-year lawsuit years later and wiped out my savings. I didn't have the courage to hold to my convictions; I had no clear boundaries. Repeatedly, I made critically bad decisions.

Just like the motorcycle accidents, the businesses were

more piled-up destruction on the side of the road. Sometimes knowingly, sometimes unknowingly, I kept up a pattern of self-sabotage. I felt unworthy of success deep inside and found ways to run from it. I didn't believe I deserved anything good.

ANN

When I think back to when I met Ann, I wonder why I thought I was ready to be married again. I still had so far to go before I was ready to be in a healthy relationship—but I didn't want to be alone. I wanted to be loved. I remember being at a seminar once and looking out at a lake outside the hotel. I saw all these ducks together, but there was one duck off by itself. I stared at it for a long time and thought, *That's me*. I didn't want to be lonely.

Ann was easy to fall in love with. She was beautiful and fun. We met at a business seminar in Peaceful Valley, Colorado; our mutual friend, Maggie, introduced us. Maggie and I knew each other from a therapy group, and Ann was in counseling at the time, too, processing her recent divorce from an abusive man. At the seminar, there was a blizzard, and we got snowed in. I did my best to charm her.

Ann initially was not enthusiastic about being charmed. She told me, "Rick, I just got divorced. Go away."

I said, "Well, if you don't want to be with me, I'll leave."

She said, "Well, leave."

Ironically, that made me determined to stay. I always liked to rise to a challenge. Ann started off being emotionally detached, and that seemed safe to me.

It took me three years to get her to marry me. Her agreement didn't come as a result of any romantic gesture of mine, or proof of my increased maturity. She went to a psychic, and the psychic said, "Look, if he won't go away, just marry him." So, she did.

There were a number of times that we could have gotten divorced, but we loved each other, and fortunately, we never wanted to leave at the same time. We also knew from our time in therapy that if we divorced before fully healing ourselves, we would probably wind up in the same spot with a different person. One thing that helped save the marriage was my travel schedule. When we got into fights, I could easily stay upset for days—even weeks. Ann would withdraw, and we'd let the anger stretch out for days. But often, I would be traveling during those stretches, and the distance worked for both of us. I'd come home from travel, we would reconnect, and then we'd be back on with each other.

The kids were also in the mix at that point. I became like

a father to Ann's children, Chris, Aaron, and later Maury, and after an initially difficult time, Mesia grew very close to Ann. Ann was great at bringing our families together. Today, we love all getting together. We also both had great therapists. I was more aware of my issues at that point—far more than I'd been with my first wife—and more willing to be vulnerable. Whatever helped us stay together, I'm so enormously grateful we stayed with it. My relationship with Ann has become a magnificent joy in my life.

BEFORE AND AFTER

Abuse left me feeling ashamed, isolated, unloved, fearful, and dead inside. Yet, at this point in my life, I am known. I am loved. I have learned to face my fears and overcome them. I've gone from a pattern of self-sabotage to understanding that I am worthy of good. I used to hate religion; now, I embrace the spark of the Divine. No longer do I self-medicate with alcohol—I drink up life itself, and it's beautiful, and there's real joy.

The rest of this book is the rest of that story—both mine and ours.

CHAPTER TWO

The Psychology and Facts of Child Abuse

Recently, I was talking to some investment bankers I know well. I was telling them about the terrible prevalence of child abuse and hoping to get their support for my nonprofit. One of them said he wanted to talk to some people about it and would get back to me.

At a follow-up meeting, this banker said, "Rick, we don't know any family that's ever experienced this. No one we know has ever dealt with abuse."

I said, "Yes, you do. But you're in the top economic echelon of society. People in your circle don't talk about it."

My friend couldn't quite grasp that—and I can't blame him. It's an ugly truth.

This book is about healing. But before I talk about healing, we need to first look at the ugly truth of where abuse survivors start. Let's be honest about the challenges that come up as a result of abuse. This chapter is going to address the facts of abuse and how its long-term effects impact our heart (emotionally) and our head (psychologically and neurologically). It all may look ugly, but it's true—and acknowledging the truth is where healing has to start.

THE FACTS: PREVALENCE OF ABUSE

Like my banker friend, we'd like to think there are certain bubbles in society where abuse doesn't occur, but statistics would prove that idea wrong. In the research I've done, I came across a quote from Ark of Hope for Children, which makes the point that "Child abuse does not discriminate based upon gender, social standing, ethnicity, or religion."[1] There is no boundary that says a child is safe in *this* economic group, or safe in *this* religious group, or at *this* social standing. Child abuse crosses every boundary and demographic.

---

[1] "Are There National Statistics about Child Abuse?" Ark of Hope for Children, July 31, 2017, https://arkofhopeforchildren.org/child-abuse/child-abuse-statistics-info.

I found different estimates about how many children are abused every year. Part of this inconsistency is because reporting requirements differ from state to state. Still, even if there was consistency across states, child abuse is not something that is reported nearly as often as it happens. Why? People don't like to talk about it. The most serious statistic—looking at child fatalities from abuse—is also probably lower than it should be. When children die from abuse, families may often request a different cause of death be noted on the death certificates.

For all these reasons, statisticians have a difficult time collecting accurate numbers about abuse, and the recent numbers available are still typically several years old. In my opinion, this is a clear indication of the fact that abused children need more people advocating on their behalf. We need to prioritize these vulnerable lives and protect them with our voice.

Here are the best numbers I could find, from the American Society for the Positive Care of Children: in 2016, it was estimated that 7.4 million children were abused.[2] Consider that: 7.4 million is roughly the population of Washington State.[3] Most of those children were abused

---

[2] "Child Abuse Statistics," American SPCC, accessed December 6, 2018, https://americanspcc.org/child-abuse-statistics/.

[3] "Washington Population 2018," World Population Review, last modified November 30, 2018, http://worldpopulationreview.com/states/washington-population/.

through neglect (74.8 percent); they were also physically abused (18.2 percent), sexually abused (8.5 percent), and/or abused in psychological ways (6.9 percent).

Most of this abuse happens within a family or close community. This is important, because when abuse happens within the family, the issue is often kept hidden. Families don't want to "air their dirty laundry" and they decide they'll deal with it privately. Most often, though, "dealing with it within the family" means *not* dealing with it. The abuser is protected from prosecution, keeping the victim in a cycle of abuse and putting more children at risk. Additionally, a third of those abused children will grow up to become abusers themselves, again continuing that vicious cycle.[4]

Given the fact that many of the most harmful effects in my own life came after being sexually abused, I was especially curious about sexual abuse statistics. The reports of sexual abuse that you often hear in the news discuss strangers abducting and hurting children, but actually, the vast majority of children are sexually abused by someone they know (90 percent). Ark of Hope for Children notes that a child is raped *every two minutes*.[5] That

---

[4] "Child Abuse Statistics," American SPCC, accessed December 6, 2018, https://americanspcc.org/child-abuse-statistics/.

[5] "Are There National Statistics about Child Abuse?" Ark of Hope for Children, July 31, 2017, https://arkofhopeforchildren.org/child-abuse/child-abuse-statistics-info.

works out to thirty rapes an hour and 720 a day—those numbers are horrifying. One in three girls will be sexually molested before age seventeen. The next time you see a gathering of children, take note of how many little girls in that group this statistic would include; one in three is a disturbingly high percentage. Among boys like me, one in every six will be molested before age seventeen. Think of a youth soccer team: two of those boys, statistically speaking, experience molestation.

The same source reports that, oftentimes, a sexually abused child is abused in other ways. If a victim of sexual abuse tries to talk about it, she may end up getting smacked or locked in a room, or being verbally abused. The same person who is willing to sexually abuse a child is usually willing to inflict a lot of additional pain.

COST TO SOCIETY

There's also a huge economic cost to child abuse. A 2012 research study estimated that child abuse costs society $124 billion annually.[6] What contributes to that enormous number? The main costs come from crime and healthcare.

The American SPCC notes that abused children are

---

[6] Richard J. Gelles and Staci Perlman, *Estimated Annual Cost of Child Abuse and Neglect* (Chicago: Prevent Child Abuse America, 2012).

approximately *nine* times more likely to get involved in criminal behavior than children who weren't abused. The website also notes, "14% of all men in prison and 36% of women in prison in the USA were abused as children, about twice the frequency seen in the general population."[7] Abuse victims also experience more social differences, which can make them feel isolated and angry.[8] They have a higher rate of continuing abusive behaviors, which continues a cycle of violence and crime.

This makes sense to me. As I discovered firsthand during my adolescence as a "hood," victims of abuse contain enormous anger, shame, and fear. Their reactions to stress can be violent. This is logical, given they've been shown a model of violence. Abuse victims also don't fully understand the connection to the action they're doing. Like I experienced, the buried pain of abuse can lead to patterns of self-sabotage where your unconscious mind makes decisions that your conscious mind would never approve of. Regardless of why it happens, the statistics make it clear: more abuse leads to more crime.

Abuse also leads to higher medical costs, in the short term and long term. It's easy enough to imagine health-

---

[7] Caroline Wolf Harlow, *Prior Abuse Reported by Inmates and Probationers* (Washington: US Department of Justice, Office of Justice Programs, 1999), http://bjs.ojp.usdoj.gov/content/pub/pdf/parip.pdf.

[8] "Are There National Statistics about Child Abuse?" Ark of Hope for Children, July 31, 2017, https://arkofhopeforchildren.org/child-abuse/child-abuse-statistics-info.

care needs for a child who's been brought to the ER after being hit—but that's only the beginning. Drug use causes no end to medical needs, and drugs share an unfortunate connection with abuse, both among abusers and abuse victims. The American SPCC says that cases of neglect have ballooned with the opioid crisis. Children who are exposed to drugs like opioids in utero are more likely to have behavioral issues and learning deficits, which creates added costs for healthcare, early intervention, and social work. Also, think of the high costs of a drug rehabilitation program—a thirty-day program can cost anywhere from $6,000 to $20,000. And what issue is at the root of two-thirds of people who are in drug rehab? Abuse.[9] As I experienced, abuse survivors often turn to self-medicating to dull the pain.

In addition to more alcoholism and drug addiction, abuse survivors have poorer physical health in general, compared to people who weren't abused.[10] Abuse survivors are much riskier in their sexual behaviors as well. Abused children are 25 percent more likely to deal with teen pregnancy and have unprotected sex, which means they're

---

[9] Neil Swan, "Exploring the Role of Child Abuse on Later Drug Abuse: Researchers Face Broad Gaps in Information," *NIDA Notes* 13, no. 2 (1998), www.nida.nih.gov/NIDA_Notes/NNVol13N2/exploring.html.

[10] Ibid.

more likely to get STDs.[11] Also, 80 percent of abuse survivors are later found to have a psychological disorder like anxiety or depression. These costs are no doubt felt personally by every abuse survivor—and their monetary cost is substantial.

Even with some of the costs noted, the "$124 billion estimated cost" number leaves out the money forfeited through a child's *lost potential*. Our children are our greatest resource. They're the future of the world. If we feed them, educate them, and nurture them, they will be able to produce far more as adults. They'll contribute more to society and spend less money on medical care, psychological care, and drug rehabilitation. Rather than cost the government money through crime, they'll be more likely to make higher incomes and contribute more taxes for society's general welfare. They may achieve higher levels of education, which could mean more advancements in cutting-edge fields.

A society without abuse would have a more productive economy and a greater GDP. There would be less hospital care and, particularly, fewer emergency room visits—think of the money that alone could save! There would be higher productivity at work and less substance abuse.

---

11 US Department of Health and Human Services, "Long-Term Consequences of Child Abuse and Neglect," Child Welfare Information Gateway, 2013, http://www.childwelfare.gov/pubs/factsheets/long_term_consequences.cfm.

The list could go on. One blogger summed up the situation well. After reviewing the costs associated with abuse, the writer states, "The economic impact of abuse is detrimental to our nation and can be clearly documented in dollars and cents; however, the immeasurable cost to a single child can never be quantified, so our investment in prevention is priceless."[12]

EMOTIONAL COST

As high a price as we pay economically for abuse, the emotional cost is even higher. The same writer, after noting the staggering economic costs related to child abuse, also made this sad evaluation: "The emotional price paid by an abused child is infinite. It is a deduction of self-esteem, trust, and faith that robs their heart's account from the moment of abuse, until a time when therapy, support, and love [may] replenish what was stolen."[13]

As horrifying as these statistics are, the whole truth is even worse. The numbers don't show the bruises, the broken bones, or the broken spirits. They don't show the deeply buried fear and terror residing in each survivor of abuse. Statistics are only words on a page—and

---

[12] "The Rising Economic Impact of Child Maltreatment," Childhelp, accessed October 18, 2018, https://www.childhelp.org/blog/cost-child-abuse-rising-economic-impact-child-maltreatment/.

[13] Ibid.

perhaps that's why so many people ignore them. If my banker friend were looking at the face of an abused child, rather than statistics, he might realize the issue is more urgent than he thought. However, those faces are largely invisible. People don't typically advertise that they are included in those statistics, acknowledging their abuse when they introduce themselves: "Hey, I'm Rick, and I was abused as a kid."

The numbers can only hint at the pain being hidden in the community around us. Laura Davis writes in *Allies in Healing*, "Child sexual abuse is a violation of power by a person with more power over someone who is more vulnerable. This violation takes a sexual form, but it involves more than sex. It involves a breach of trust, a breaking of boundaries and a profound violation of the survivor's sense of self."[14]

Broken trust; broken boundaries; a violation of not only the body, but the soul. Abuse has a cost, all right. What a profound understatement. People typically think of abuse showing up in bruises and scars, but the emotional scars can be far more painful and long-lasting. Here's what some of those look like:

---

14   Laura Davies, *Allies in Healing* (New York: Harper Collins, 1993).

Emotional Effects:[15]

- Lack of trust
- Inability to engage in fulfilling relationships
- Feeling "too damaged to love"
- Low self-worth or feelings of worthlessness
- Difficulties with controlling emotions
- Depression, anxiety, and anger
- Suicidal thoughts and behaviors

The list of emotional effects is long—but probably not long enough to accurately reflect all the ways a child suffers emotional scars from abuse. Much of these effects tie into the point noting "low self-worth." After my experience being abused, I felt too damaged to love. That low self-worth led me to take all the risks that nearly killed me: the drugs, the car accidents, the motorcycle accidents. Even worse, low self-esteem can lead many victims of abuse to consider suicide or go so far as to commit it.

The most tragic effects of abuse end in death. Children may die from violence or choose to commit suicide because of the incredible pain they suffer. Around 1,850 children a year die from some form of child abuse—that

---

[15] "Effects, Signs & Symptoms of Physical & Sexual Abuse," Ascent Children's Health Services, accessed October 2, 2018, http://www.ascentchs.com/mental-health/child-abuse/symptoms-signs-effects/.

equals seven or more children *a day*.[16] Young children are the most vulnerable; most of those deaths from abuse (80 percent) happen to children under the age of four. Just as tragic, if not more so, approximately six children will commit suicide *every day* due to child abuse.[17]

Suicide can be prominent among children and adolescents; they may not have the ability or maturity to think the pain might lessen or that they can heal. The abuse impacts their lives over and over, and they give up. This is heartbreaking—but these numbers may even be minimized because of inaccurate death certificates. When a child is killed because of violence, the death certificate may not reflect how that death actually occurred. It may be hard to prove the actual cause of death, and few families will volunteer the true cause if it could result in a family member being prosecuted. Inaccurate reporting adds to the tragedy of a child's death. It can prevent needed change from happening that would help protect children in the future.

THE ROLE OF DENIAL IN PERPETUATING THE CYCLE

Issues like inaccurate reporting make child abuse look

---

16 "Are There National Statistics about Child Abuse?" Ark of Hope for Children, July 31, 2017, https://arkofhopeforchildren.org/child-abuse/child-abuse-statistics-info.

17 Ibid

like a smaller issue than it is. It's not just problems with cause-of-death reports. Different forms of denial also keep the issue hidden.

When there was a shooting at Marjory Stoneman Douglas High School in Florida, there was news coverage of the shooting every night. It created a national outrage. So many people were caught up by the students and their stories that a movement was started, funding was raised, and momentum was built towards change.

Abuse doesn't get reported every night. We hear about the most extreme cases, when a child is attacked by a stranger or even killed. That gets outrage, and rightly so. But when a family man with a nice job comes home and sexually molests his daughter, very few people know. The mother may know but not do anything, because she's also afraid. If the child does speak up, there's a strong incentive to doubt her story. The tendency is to shut that child up or say, "Oh, she wants attention."

Another form of denial is acting like sexual abuse is no big deal. Dan A. Turner became infamous after he published a letter defending his son, Brock Turner, who was convicted of raping a fellow Stanford student. After his son was sentenced to six months of jail time, Dan Turner complained, "That is a steep price to pay for 20 minutes of action."[18] Brock assaulted his victim behind a dumpster and left her bleeding in multiple places, yet his father had the gall to minimize it by calling rape "20 minutes of action." What he meant was twenty minutes of beating and sexually violating a woman.

Assault gets denied, covered up, and hidden. When it does get spoken of, people often brush it off. They may say the victim was exaggerating, or they'll question the victim's character. They downplay the abuse. They dismiss it as "locker-room talk." As a result of all this denial, perpetrators continue to abuse the vulnerable, with no accountability.

Abusers don't just abuse their victims; they also abuse power. The Hollywood producer Harvey Weinstein abused women for years using his power. He had the power to ruin careers and people's lives. He had the power to hire the best attorneys and hire investigators to find ways to smear his victims. He had the power to intimidate. Victims of abuse are afraid to lose their job or position. Abusers use this fear to manipulate their victims into silence.

---

18   Michael E. Miller, "'A Steep Price to Pay for 20 Minutes of Action': Dad Defends Stanford Sex Offender," *Washington Post*, June 6, 2016, https://www.washingtonpost.com/news/morning-mix/wp/2016/06/06/a-steep-price-to-pay-for-20-minutes-of-action-dad-defends-stanford-sex-offender/?utm_term=.839da5950d9e.

Some perpetrators use a sick, twisted message of love to attract their victims and keep them in the net. This may be especially true with pedophiles. Abusers can be charismatic people and will strategically establish a close relationship with a child. When the abuse finally starts, they've put themselves in a position of power over the child through "love," like Bob did with me. Their demands for secrecy are agreed to because the child doesn't feel strong enough to rebel against such a trusted adult.

The abuser's ability to manipulate, hide, and charm a child's caretaker can also contribute to denial. Larry Nassar was the US women's Olympic gymnastics team's sports medicine doctor and was found to have sexually abused more than 150 victims during the years he was treating gymnasts. Unbelievably, he committed most of his abuse while parents were in the room, covering girls with a towel or having them wear loose basketball shorts. While carrying on casual conversation with the parents, he would be abusing the girls under the loose fabric. Although several of the girls spoke up, parents didn't want to believe such a horrifying thing was happening under their watch.[19] Nassar was clever, manipulative, and charismatic—as are many abusers.

---

19 Christine Hauser, "At Larry Nassar's Sentencing, Parents Ask: 'How Did I Miss the Red Flags?'" *New York Times*, January 24, 2018, https://www.nytimes.com/2018/01/24/sports/larry-nassar-parents.html.

Especially when abuse occurs within a family, denial can be common and particularly tragic. Children are more inclined to stay silent if a family member is abusing them, due to their sense of family loyalty. Even if a child does speak up, denial may be at work. No one wants to believe their child is being abused, especially not by a beloved and trusted family member. If a child reports abuse, but the abuser denies it, parents may choose to believe that the child was simply confused. Remember: abusers are charismatic and manipulative. They're brilliant at deflecting blame. Tragically, this keeps kids in a cycle of abuse and results in overwhelming feelings of guilt for parents if and when the abuse is finally exposed.

LONG-TERM EMOTIONAL EFFECTS OF ABUSE

The emotional cost of abuse can last far beyond the weeks and months after the actual experience. As I experienced in my own life, there are many long-term effects of abuse, which can interfere with an abuse survivor's ability to live a full and productive life. These effects can also serve as warning signs that point to repressed trauma. Some of these long-term effects have such a profound and long-lasting impact, they're worth looking at more closely.

WORTHLESSNESS

Imagine a young girl who experiences regular sexual

abuse by her father. The man who raised her is supposed to love and protect her. But instead of providing care, he's violating her. How is she supposed to stand up to that? Children and even teenagers look up to their parents, so if a primary caretaker is abusing them, they accept the message that they're not worthy of genuine love.

One of the women I got to know through therapy was raped for a number of years by her father, her uncle, and two in-laws. The reasoning they gave her was that she was too beautiful. They couldn't help it, they said. It was her fault. The message they gave her about her core identity was that she was there for them to screw. They gave her no choice in the matter.

When an adult takes control of a child or a weaker person, the abuser takes away the victim's power. If you're the one being abused, you end up feeling like you're not worth anything; you're just being used for sexual pleasure and used brutally. You conclude that you have no more worth than an object—because if you *were* a worthwhile, loving human being, you wouldn't have been used like that. Caretakers are supposed to help children grow, thrive, and develop their confidence and skills. When caretakers abuse children rather than care for them, the opposite effect occurs: abusers teach their victims that they have no worth.

SELF-SABOTAGE

As I've described in my own story, I developed a pattern of self-sabotage based on the belief that I didn't deserve anything good. For years, I had financial failure after failure; I had a long history of alcohol abuse; I repeatedly ran from relationships or challenging jobs. Eventually, I began to wake up to the fact that I was sabotaging myself.

It was devastating to realize how I had taken over from the abuser and started abusing myself, subconsciously. I had to challenge deep-seated, learned behavior. I had to *unlearn* all of my negative beliefs and challenge everything in my mind. I had to remember the truth of who I was.

This can be a common experience among abuse survivors. Victims will uncover mental challenges where they hit walls and must examine deep-seated, learned behavior. These learned behaviors can perpetuate "self-abuse." One woman I knew from a therapy group would get into relationships that she described as always starting off wonderful. In a matter of months, she'd tell us the guy had begun slapping her around. This woman was continually attracted to abusive men, and not only that, the codependent behavior she'd learned made her provoke them. None of the men had any right to hurt her—let's make that clear. But because of her own negative beliefs about herself, she would bait these men until they snapped and confirmed her fears.

Both this woman and I realized we had to take some personal responsibility for the sabotage we were bringing on ourselves. I remember concluding that I had to stop looking outside myself to get healed. It had to come from within me.

THE SOUL AND HEART ARE BROKEN

When you are abused, especially by a loved one, the heart gets broken. Emotions suddenly become dangerous because you're feeling so much pain. You can't allow yourself to be sensitive to pain, which means you shut down your ability to be sensitive to anyone. You lose the power to feel love, compassion, or empathy.

After the summer I experienced abuse, my major goal was *to not feel*. Alcohol became my friend, but it ultimately became my enemy. The methods I used to deaden my feelings made me disconnected and insensitive. When you stop feeling negative emotions, you end up stopping yourself from feeling everything. You lose the ability to be emotionally intimate and feel sensitivity for a person you love.

PSYCHOLOGICAL AND NEUROLOGICAL EFFECTS

Long-term effects from abuse don't just show up on an emotional level; they also impact the brain and psyche.

I've said for years that abuse "rewires" the brain, but I didn't realize how true that was until I began doing the research for this book. Abuse survivors have different psychological and neurological characteristics than people who have never been abused. As I described in the last chapter, some of the psychological changes I experienced after abuse were low self-esteem and a self-destructive personality. I made reckless decisions without thinking of the consequences. It turns out those are all common trends among abuse victims.

The British newspaper *The Guardian* reported on some of the neurological changes that can occur in abuse victims:

> Three key areas of the hippocampus in the brain were smaller in people who reported maltreatment in childhood. Being sexually or emotionally abused as a child can affect the development of a part of the brain that controls **memory** and the **regulation of emotions**, a study suggests. The results add to the growing body of evidence that childhood abuse raises the **risk of mental illness, such as depression, personality disorders, and anxiety** well into adulthood.[20] (Emphasis added)

The natural order of a child's mind is destroyed when

---

20 Alok Jha, "Childhood Abuse May Stunt Growth of Part of Brain Involved in Emotions," *Guardian*, February 13, 2012, https://www.theguardian.com/science/2012/feb/13/childhood-abuse-growth-brain-emotions.

they're abused, especially sexually. I missed out completely on a normal experience with sexual development. Most teenagers date, kiss, pet, and so on, progressing at their own pace. I had no choice about when I was introduced to sex, and the way I was introduced to it was perverted. I had a horrible sense of what sex should be. That's only one area of the brain that can be impacted by abuse, but the quote above suggests that the "rewiring" goes way beyond just sexual development.

Abuse damages the biological functioning of a child's mind. The Dana Foundation, a well-respected institute sponsoring mental health research, published this comment:

> We easily understand how beating a child may damage the developing brain, but what about the all-too-common psychological abuse of children? Because the abuse was not physical, these children may be told, as adults, that they should "just get over it." But...scientists are discovering some startling connections between abuse of all kinds and both **permanent and debilitating changes in the brain and psychiatric problems, ranging from panic attacks to posttraumatic stress disorder.**[21] (Emphasis added)

---

21   Martin H. Teicher, "Wounds That Time Won't Heal: The Neurobiology of Child Abuse," Dana Foundation, October 1, 2000, http://www.dana.org/Cerebrum/2000/Wounds_That_Time_Won't_Heal__The_Neurobiology_of_Child_Abuse/.

Given some of these neurological changes, children suffering from the effects of abuse may have the odds stacked against them in more ways than one. Research shows that abuse survivors can experience impaired brain development, poor emotional and mental health, and cognitive difficulties.[22] Think of how those challenges could compound. In my life, the stutter I developed after abuse made me reluctant to ever volunteer in class. When I did speak up, the stutter made my teachers assume I was mentally delayed. I was put into lower-level classes and didn't receive the same educational opportunities that my peers did. Perhaps I would have struggled in school anyway, but who knows what my academic experience would have looked like if I hadn't been abused.

Many of these neurological changes are easily seen when you consider some of the common reactions to abuse among children.

COMMON REACTIONS

Abused children experience the unthinkable. There's no way for a child to comprehend why he would have been singled out for such harm, so a child's brain processes the abuse in a variety of ways.

---

[22] "Are There National Statistics about Child Abuse?" Ark of Hope for Children, July 31, 2017, https://arkofhopeforchildren.org/child-abuse/child-abuse-statistics-info.

Confusion may come first—you can't understand why you're being hurt by someone who is supposed to love you.

Shame may come next, as you conclude the abuse must have somehow been your fault.

Repression may trump them all when memories are so painful the brain simply won't allow them into the conscious mind.

Each of these reactions is important to look at in order to understand what abuse survivors need to heal from.

I've experienced all of these reactions, as I shared in the previous chapter. Below I share anonymous testimonies from other abuse survivors to provide a fuller picture of how these reactions can look.

Confusion and Lack of Comprehension

I never knew my real father. My mother and her sister felt it was too shameful to let me know my mom wasn't sure who got her pregnant. I didn't learn this for many years.

When I was a kid, around four or five, my mom dropped me off at my daycare center. But she never came back. She just left me there, thinking this woman who owned the daycare could take better care of me. But she was wrong. She was so very wrong.

> The oldest son of the daycare owner started sexually molesting me for years. As I reached my preteens, I started acting out. They decided I was too much to handle, so they took me back to my mom.
>
> Can you imagine the reality of being given away and then given away again? I felt like I didn't belong there. I felt like I didn't belong anywhere. I felt like I didn't belong to anyone. No one talked about where I had been or why I had been abandoned. As I grew into a teenager, my uncle molested me.
>
> Living between two worlds, I did my best to fit in, because I wanted to belong somewhere, anywhere.[23]

This young lady was abandoned twice, then subjected to years of abuse. After removal from her first abusive context, she was put in another abusive context. Confusion was everywhere. Where could she go? Who was her ally? Whom could she talk to about any of it? This is a kid who wanted to belong anywhere—but she had no idea where to find that belonging. She wanted to be loved—but had no idea what love looked like. Instead of experiencing a loving adult's protection, she experienced repeated sexual abuse by someone bigger and older than she was.

Abuse and maltreatment like this wreaks havoc on a

---

23 Testimonies provided by Randa Fox, director of Not on Our Watch America Foundation, July 26, 2018.

child's mind. The confusion that goes along with abuse threatens the most basic ideas of who we are. When I was a kid, I felt unloved for most of my childhood. Then Bob showed up and gave me the attention I'd always wanted. He was fun, he was a cop, he got along with my parents—he was my hero. He earned my trust and love and made me feel like I had real worth. But then he took that trust and my need for him and used it for his own sexual gratification. I couldn't put that together in my head. I didn't know who I was; I didn't know how to understand Bob; I couldn't understand what was happening in my body—I couldn't comprehend any of it.

Shame and Blame

I will never forget what my father told me as a young boy. He said, "Son, you are a man now. Men don't cry. Men never show weakness, ever. You must be strong and brave and fearless."

How could I tell him that, at the age of thirteen, I had already failed? I had already disappointed my father. An uncle, whom I loved, had been molesting me since I was eight. My uncle told me that because my body responded to his advances that I must have liked it. I must have wanted it. And he even told me it was my fault. That I had somehow tempted him. I carried that blame around for more years than I care to admit.

Of course, I know now that is was NEVER my fault. I know now

> that men do cry, and men can be vulnerable and show emotion. I knew that any blame belonged squarely on the shoulders of the man who committed the crime against me. I never told anyone until years later, when my life was falling apart and I couldn't understand why. Thanks to a great therapist and a support group for Adult Survivors of Child Abuse, I am able to give my children the kind of safe, stable, nurturing environment that every child needs to thrive.

A child is innocent and defenseless. Unlike most animals, who launch their young out into the world within a year, human babies take a long time to mature. For many years, they're vulnerable; they don't have the information they need to fend for themselves. Children are born expecting to be loved and cared for, to be at their mother's nurturing breast.

Abuse rips all of that away. Abuse denies children their protection, their nurturing environment, and most of all, their innocence. Can you imagine being in this abuse survivor's position, as an eight-year-old boy? He was abused by his uncle and then told by his father that he could never cry or be vulnerable. His abuser robbed him of his innocence and put the blame for his horrible act on the boy. He was then made to feel even more shame by his father's unintentional rebuke.

A pedophile told lies to this boy in order to place his

own guilt onto an innocent child. Over and over, abused children are blamed; they're made to feel they did something wrong. The predators who abuse them do this to justify their own criminal behavior. And, because abuse victims are looking for a reason to understand *why* they were abused, they accept the explanation that it was their fault.

If you are reading this and recognize similar feelings of blame and shame in yourself, you need to know two crucial things. One: you're not alone. Two—and this is critical—it was not your fault. Many sexually abused victims have tremendous guilt over having an orgasm, but that's not a choice. That's a physiological response. In rape, a woman's vagina creates fluid; this happens not from enjoyment, but for protection. The body naturally does that to protect the internal sexual organs. I remember a conversation with one abuse survivor who was over fifty years old. We were discussing the abuse she experienced years ago, and she said, "I still can't understand why I had an orgasm."

I learned there isn't a choice about how your body responds during abuse. Something like an orgasm is a biological, physiological response to stimulation—even stimulation that is unwelcome. Abuse survivors need to understand you did nothing wrong. Even more importantly, you can heal, no matter what happened.

Repression

I was the youngest of four. My dad was in the Navy and was mean. I was so afraid of him. He used to hit my older brother and sisters with a board. He didn't hit me with a board. He did knock the shit out of me twice with his hands.

I remember one day when we lived in Hawaii; I was between the third and sixth grade. I was sitting on my bunk bed, playing with my new tape recorder, when my dad walked in. He had on a white terry cloth robe, and he picked me up. He never said a word. I just knew I wanted to sit on my bed and play with my recorder. I can remember seeing him carry me, my little legs dangling, as he walked with me into the living room. He laid me down on the green carpet that was so popular in the late 1960s. And then I don't remember anything...Until I got up and touched a wet spot on the carpet. I went and laid on the couch, feeling very bad.

At the age of fifteen, I had attempted suicide. After I got out of the ICU, I was placed in a private room. I remember falling asleep watching Johnny Carson on the Tonight Show. *I awoke feeling that someone had been touching me between my legs. There was a policeman in my room. He asked me why I was there, but I was too embarrassed to tell him. He said he had already read my chart. He talked to me for a long time, and when he got up to leave, he asked for a kiss. Then he French-kissed me.*

I always knew that these two incidents were connected. It wasn't until I was twenty-one years old, when my oldest sister called me and asked me if our dad had ever sexually molested me, that the light bulb turned on. I finally had a name for what had happened to me. To this day, I have been unable to remember exactly what my father did to me. But through my two older sisters, I know that he had abused me.

An experience of abuse like this causes so much horror, such massive terror, that the mind blanks it out completely. As a form of protection, the memory is repressed; it is far too painful for a child to understand.

This young woman was abused by her father, someone who was supposed to protect her. The depression and pain that followed was so extreme, it led her to attempt suicide. She was already carrying tremendous pain, and then a policeman—again, someone who was supposed to protect her—abused her while she was alone in a private room, with no recourse. Imagine the pain, humiliation, desperation, and confusion. The conscious mind simply cannot deal with that much terror.

Abuse victims don't want to feel the pain of their attack through relived memories—so the mind shuts off. It stops. I repressed my memories of abuse for years, until extensive counseling drew them out of me. But even so, the memory of going to Bob's neighbor's house and being alone with two men remains a black spot in my mind. The mind is a powerful instrument; it can make you believe nothing ever happened.

OTHER LONG-TERM PSYCHOLOGICAL EFFECTS

Confusion, shame, repression, increased anxiety, PTSD, depression, an impact on memory and emotional regulation...These are just some of the ways that abuse can rewire a person's thinking. As you'd expect, there's a ripple effect from some of these changes. They can end up impacting many other areas of your life, from your relationships to your career.

Failed Relationships

Many of the long-term psychological effects from abuse may impact relationships with friends or romantic partners. I've already described some of the fears I took into relationships—when they got intimate, I got scared. I also had to deal with the sexual perversions and fantasies that got into my mind from the pornography I was shown. Those images flooded in when I was with a woman and made me scared.

Increased anxiety, depression, low self-esteem, a pattern of self-sabotage—all these struggles may affect an abuse survivor's relationships. They may get in the way of healthy intimacy and connection or prevent you from embracing a good thing.

Business and Financial Problems

Psychological effects from abuse can sneak into your job performance as well. Imagine you're an abuse survivor prone to anxiety, and you get a panic attack right before a presentation. Your job performance suddenly takes a nosedive, which may stir up more feelings of shame, which can lead to more anxiety, and so on. The effects follow us into the office. Particularly because of the stress that many people experience at work, negative effects from abuse can easily be triggered.

In my case, I made bad economic decisions. I was attracted to crazy financial deals and didn't do research. I was easily persuaded by charismatic people. I was successful often enough that I'd like to think I had good instincts for my field—but usually, the demons I carried from abuse led me to sabotage my own best efforts. Many abuse survivors may have similar stories to share.

Isolation and Loneliness

Abuse survivors may also deal with a crippling sense of isolation. The abuse is the first instance when you're isolated. Then, you're further cut off from others because there's no one you feel that you can talk to about it. I'll never forget Bob's words to me: "This is so special between us, and you can *never, ever* talk to anyone about it." Abusers like to use their authority to intimidate a more vulnerable person into secrecy, and then the vulnerable person has nowhere to go with it. They become alone.

Shame requires three things: secrecy, silence, and judgment.

Secrecy is formed when the abuser pressures their victim to never tell what happened.

Silence comes next; you can't talk about it.

Judgment arrives on its heels, because the abuser makes the child believe they did something wrong.

The combination creates shame, and when you carry shame, you don't feel great about meeting other people. You always are afraid that someone is going to find you out. You can't love yourself, so you believe no one else could love you either. The result is profound isolation and loneliness; it destroys trust and perverts love.

YOU CAN HEAL AND CHANGE

In my own story, I experienced a major self-destructive

streak because of some of those psychological changes. I always say, "When the abuser stops, the abused takes over and abuses themselves." Our brains get so messed up by abuse that we start ruining our own lives.

I have one thing to say to that: the abuse was not your fault.

No matter what happened, it was not your fault. You don't have to recreate abuse in your life to punish yourself. Your brain and mine may have been rewired by abuse, but we can *change our minds*. It is possible for every abuse survivor to overcome the damage caused emotionally and psychologically by abuse. You can heal!

The rest of this book focuses on ways you can do that. I've shared my story of abuse and the ways it damaged my life. Now, I want to tell you the ways I found my way back to the light. The journey took years, and it wasn't easy, but it was worth every challenging step.

Brené Brown writes, "Owning our story can be hard, but not nearly as difficult as spending our lives running from it. Embracing our vulnerabilities is risky, but not nearly as dangerous as giving up on love and belonging and joy—the experiences that make us the most vulnerable. Only when we are brave enough to explore the darkness will we discover the infinite power of our light."

Somewhere mixed up with the memories of abuse, mixed up with the emotional and psychological damage, I think there's something always within us looking for good. We don't know what it is, but it's there: something that can help touch a light within us. It wants us to open ourselves to the possibility that there is good and we are allowed to explore it.

The abused know the darkness. It pervades us. It hovers around us. It is waiting for more. *But it does not need to defeat us.*

Listen to the power within you that wants to discover the good—the deep good, the true good, the whole good. If you can, you can come to live an incredibly joyful, productive, and fulfilling life. You can learn to love and be loved.

CHAPTER THREE

My Story Continues: Healing

For so long, I believed I would never heal. I didn't even have "healing" as a concept in my mind. I thought, "This is the way I am, and this is the way I'll always be." I dealt with tragedy after tragedy, bringing more misfortune on myself and others. I was always waiting for the other shoe to drop—so it always did.

When life finally took me to rock bottom, I had to conclude that something was not right. The pain got so severe that my choices seemed to be either commit suicide or do something very, very different.

Here's what I discovered: the only obstacle to healing—both yours and mine—is the mind. I *believed* that I was stuck, and so I remained stuck.

IT'S POSSIBLE TO HEAL FROM ABUSE

People who have experienced abuse may have a mentality that expects the worst. They may be judgmental of themselves and others. But when you embrace the identity of a resilient person, you pivot. You say, "I can and I will heal. I don't know how, but I know that I can begin this journey."

When I opened myself up to the idea that I could heal, the Universe seemed to help me along. Positive messages and strategies started coming in my direction, and for once, I didn't reject them; instead, I started to listen closely and bring them in.

When you make a commitment to heal, you open yourself up to good gifts from within. Instead of saying "This is horrible," you look around and say "This is beautiful." Your heart and your perspective become more open to acts of kindness and compassion. That sets you up for a wonderful exchange, because when you extend kindness, you experience kindness and compassion in return. More and more good begins to flow towards you.

This is a choice you must make; you must genuinely

commit yourself to do the hard work of healing. However, it's not a choice you need to make alone.

Deep inside each one of us, there is a spark that will always be connected to goodness and truth. Some people call this the Holy Spirit; some people call it a Divine Presence; some people recognize the spark simply as an innate desire to heal and love. It is this spark that makes us resilient, that makes it possible for us to heal. There's the story of a Rwandan orphan, Justus Uwayesu, who lived in a garbage dump in Kigali. He scrounged through trash for food and slept with three other children in a burned-out car. When he encountered an aid worker at age nine, he hadn't bathed for a year. The other children she approached scattered, but Justus stood his ground and told her he wanted to go to school. She was able to help him. Years later, his story was published in *The New York Times* after he got a full-tuition scholarship to attend Harvard. *The Times* wrote, "He is an example of the potential buried even in humanity's most hopeless haunts, and a sobering reminder of how seldom it is mined."[1]

That's resilience. Your mind may dwell in the equivalent of a burned-out car in a garbage dump. That's certainly

---

[1] Michael Wines, "From a Rwandan Dump to the Halls of Harvard," *New York Times*, October 23, 2014, https://www.nytimes.com/2014/10/23/us/from-a-rwandan-dump-to-the-halls-of-harvard.html.

where mine used to be, but it doesn't have to stay there. This young boy, Justus, listened to the spark inside of him—the spark of hope, the spark of his own potential.

That spark is always waiting for us to listen. When we do, it becomes possible to relearn the truth of who we are: we were created by a bountiful and giving Divine Presence, and we each carry the Divine within us. When I began to listen to that spark, I was able to wake up to wonder and beauty. It had always surrounded me, but I'd never seen it.

Listen to that spark: you have the power within you to heal. You did nothing wrong. You were innocent. You were a loving, beautiful, trusting child. That trust was shattered, and that was not your fault. Know that you are resilient and that you have the power to heal.

Maybe that feels hard to believe. I've listened to plenty of people who don't know there's a way out—but that's why I want to share my story with you. I came from horrible abuse, yet I healed. I'm now living a productive life in a fabulous relationship. Rather than expecting bad to flood my way, I expect good things. A sign hanging in my office reads, "Nothing without joy." It reminds me that it is my divine right to have joy in my life.

Of course, it took me a long time before I believed that.

MY STORY OF HEALING

By the 1980s, I had one failed marriage and a second marriage experiencing severe difficulty. I did not want to get divorced again—for my sake, for Ann's sake, and for the sake of my daughter and Ann's three kids. So I started to seek out help.

I flew all over the country trying healing practices, spiritual self-help seminars, doing bodywork, and so on. They all offered something helpful; for instance, the first regular counseling work I did helped heal me from my recurring nightmares. After that therapy, I concluded, "Great! I've got it." But I'd only *begun* to "get it"—that initial work only scratched the surface. I never dealt with the sexual abuse, and I didn't seek out therapists who had experience working with abuse victims.

When you're abused, you have a tendency to seek out negative experiences to confirm your worst suspicions. I often left bodywork sessions feeling physically good, but my mind still operated with negative beliefs. I still made bad decisions because I didn't believe I deserved anything truly good. None of these therapies had changed my basic programming or my default assumptions about what I did or didn't deserve.

Healing requires a change in belief, which comes from within. I kept looking outside myself to get healed—and that didn't work. It's only when I went *inside* that healing truly began.

BEAUTIFUL BEULAH

Beulah Clay Edmonds was a key person who helped me heal on that deep inward level. I met Beulah when I was visiting my good friend John in Eureka Springs, Arkansas. He had just gotten married to a wonderful woman, Rebecca. Rebecca was a joy to be around—and powerful. She was a bodyworker who was strong enough to break you in half and not the kind of woman you could easily say no to.

While I was visiting, Rebecca informed me, "Rick, we're going to go to church on Sunday." I protested and made excuses. After my upbringing, church was one of the last places I ever wanted to go. But Rebecca insisted—so I went.

Oak Hill Church was right on the Missouri–Arkansas border. It was a tiny place, with probably fourteen people attending. When I entered, I saw a little old lady who looked close to a hundred years old, and she was beaming. This was Beulah. She was the minister.

Rebecca introduced me. Beulah looked me in the eyes and said, "I'm glad you're here, Rick. I need a Sunday school teacher, and I don't have one today. So you're going to teach Sunday school."

I said, "I don't think that's a good idea."

Beulah replied, "Well, I think it is. And I think you'll do a wonderful job."

The Pentecostal service started out with a lengthy stretch of singing. Then Beulah cheerfully instructed me to take the kids back to an adjacent room. I knew a lot of the Bible because of my upbringing, although I didn't believe in any of it at the time. Still, as I faced the kids gathered in front of me, they looked back at me with these eager, wonderful smiles. I can still picture their faces: the brightness, the eagerness, the innocence. They were so beautiful, I couldn't help but give the Sunday school lesson my best shot. It went well, and the kids seemed to like it.

We returned to the service, at which point I had my first experience with Pentecostal prayers. Everyone in the church held hands in a circle, and Beulah began praying in tongues. I thought, "Holy smokes—where are the rattlesnakes?" In spite of my skepticism, though, the experience touched something deep within me. I listened to Beulah pray and saw that she experienced peacefulness, trust, and a faith that I had never known. I thought, "I like being around this lady."

I started flying up there simply to spend time with John, Rebecca, and Beulah. She inspired me. As a minister and a midwife, she believed so strongly in being guided by the Lord that she never questioned if she felt compelled to go somewhere. Even if she had no money—and they never had much money—she was always provided for, somehow. She didn't think it would happen—she *knew* it would happen. That amazed me.

Growing up, religion had been something that I *did*. But the power that Beulah believed in defined her from the heart. Her faith had compassion, care for others, love, and a powerful belief.

I began to realize there might be power in faith. It was something that I had totally rejected for most of my life. Beulah didn't bring me back to religion, but she did bring me back to believing in a Divine Presence. I began to have hope that there was a power beyond myself, and I wanted more of it.

ANN'S SINGING

In 2011, I was under a huge amount of stress. There were lawsuits filed against me, and I was reeling from a business failure. On top of all that, I was experiencing the worst back pain of my life. The kids and grandkids were visiting for Christmas, but I could hardly get out of bed. Going to the bathroom was excruciating, and taking a shower was even worse. I'd get in, wash up, and then throw myself on the bed, still wet, because I couldn't stand.

Hoping it might help, a friend had given me a book called *The Mindbody Prescription*, by Dr. John Sarno, from the New York University Medical Center.[2] Dr. Sarno posits a theory that pain is a result of unconscious rage. I skimmed the book but didn't do any of the exercises. Nevertheless, I was intrigued.

One night, I was sprawled on the living room couch while my wife, Ann, practiced her singing. She's classically trained, and I've always loved listening to her sing. As I lay there, feeling struck by the beauty of her voice, I suddenly realized I had absolutely no pain. I felt perfectly normal. As soon as I realized it, the pain came flooding back in.

A light bulb turned on. *Something had happened in my mind.* I could have ignored it or told myself I'd imagined the relief. Instead, I went and got *The Mindbody Prescription*. I read it obsessively for nearly a week. I did all the exercises, and the pain started to subside.

---

[2] John E. Sarno, *The Mindbody Prescription: Healing the Body, Healing the Pain* (New York: Warner Books, 1999).

ACTIVELY LOOKING WITHIN

Around that time I went into a clinic for a pre-op appointment for a scheduled back surgery. Normally when I went into the clinic, I'd scream the whole time from the pain. I'm sure I was their favorite patient! At this checkup, though, the pain had noticeably subsided. The doctor said, "Rick, you've got some movement here. What happened?" I told him I wasn't sure, but that I was starting to feel better.

He said, "Let's put the surgery off a couple weeks and watch this. Let's see what happens."

After two weeks, I was up moving and walking around. The doctor said, "Rick, I don't see any reason to do surgery. Start golfing. Do whatever you want. If you blow it up, I'll fix it." His assessment seemed to confirm that the pain I'd been feeling originated from my subconscious mind. I had emotional anguish stored deep inside me, and my body had hidden that anguish with physical pain. It had distracted me from thinking about the tragic experiences in my past and all my current stress. But—I began to believe—if I could target the pain in my subconscious mind, I could heal.

For the first time in my life, I began actively looking within.

I'd spent most of my life trying not to feel pain. I drank

alcohol, did drugs, and pursued reckless adrenaline rushes—all to avoid feeling pain. Unfortunately, when I chose to not feel negative things, I basically chose to not feel at all. My subconscious mind didn't distinguish between emotions; there wasn't a way I could manage to only feel the good stuff.

Fears grow when you never deal with them. If you continue to fight them, you have to keep pushing them down until they're buried deep. That's when they turn into demons. Or, in other words, that's when fear starts to control your decisions. The demons grow stronger and gain power as you reject them. Eventually, those demons become powerful enough that they can swing your life way off course. The buried pain leaks out in many different ways.

I used to let things build up and then I'd explode in anger. I'd get drunk and go driving. I suffered from crippling back pain. Those buried demons were determined to leak out.

In order to destroy them, I had to learn to welcome those demons. I had to let them come up out of my subconscious mind and into my conscious mind. The feelings were painful. However, as I let the feelings move from my subconscious to my conscious mind and fully felt them, the buried pain and fear began to dissolve.

There's a cartoon I like that pictures a guy in bed, crunched up against the headboard, the blanket pulled tight around his neck. There's this big, ugly demon at the end of the bed. The guy says, "What are you going to do with me?" The demon looks at him and says, "Well, the real question is, what do you want me to do with you? This is your dream, you know."[3]

There are demons. We create them. We nurture them, and we've got to release them. When light is shone upon them, they lose their power. I share more about my methods of shining that light in chapter 5.

MANKIND PROJECT

Around the same time I read *The Mindbody Prescription*, I attended a spiritual healing retreat and finally confronted my history of sexual abuse. The retreat was helpful, but it was a one-time experience—and ideally, I was looking for more. I'd met a friend at the seminar, Bill Stanley, who seemed honorable and trustworthy. Bill told me about a men's group called ManKind Project and suggested it might help me continue the healing I'd started.

Initially, the thought of joining a men's group did not appeal to me. I generally felt unsafe around groups of

---

[3] Ernest Holmes, *Living the Science of the Mind* [audiobook] (Golden, CO: Science of Mind Publishing, 2012.

men because of my history with sexual abuse. I Googled "ManKind Project" to get a better sense of what this group was about. Their website had plenty of interesting material, but I found some concerning posts too. One discussion forum called it a cult. I went back to Bill and his colleague Matt Kelly with questions.

Matt pointed out that ManKind's purpose is to help each individual man discover his *own* mission, whereas cults usually revolve around the agenda of a single charismatic leader. The groups are peer-led and meet in twenty-two countries around the world. ManKind Project is a nonprofit training and educational organization that hosts personal development programs for men—and they have decades of proven success. As I would later find out, these groups are often life-changing. Men are supported in living lives that are more authentic, service-oriented, and characterized by integrity. Their whole deal, Matt told me, "is to heal the world one man, one father, one husband at a time."

I'd asked my questions and felt satisfied with the answers. Plus, Bill was persistent. He kept calling me up and inviting me to attend a group. Finally, I gave it a try.

At my first meeting, I didn't do anything but listen. There were ground rules; confidentiality was big. Outside of the group, you were free to share your own story, but you couldn't share anyone else's, unless you had their permission. When a man spoke, he was not to be interrupted. He held the floor until he explicitly said "I'm done." Even if he was silent for two minutes, working through stuff in his head, everyone was still expected to listen respectfully until he was ready to continue or he said he was done.

One of the men discussed some significant problems in his marriage. He was emotional when he talked about the marriage breaking up and got pretty vulnerable when sharing about the ways he was contributing to the dysfunction. It wasn't pretty, but no one interrupted; no one said, "Dude, that's nasty." They just attentively listened. When the man finished sharing, there were no comments other than "Would you like feedback?" That was the case for every man who shared, and the man could say yes or no. If he said yes, the other men would courteously give input.

I was amazed by how respectful the men were of each other. I'd never been in a company of men like that, and I felt a safety among them that I'd never experienced before. Bill was right; this was an ideal place to begin to unpack some of my repressed memories.

When I first shared about the sexual abuse, I braced myself for rejection—but there was no negative response. I began to realize I wasn't the only one there dealing with past abuse; I wasn't *alone*. At ManKind Project, I could talk about it and not be judged; instead, I was actually loved. That was incredible.

As I shared about my past, those demons in my subconscious started to lose their power. As I've said, in order to survive, shame requires secrecy, silence, and judgment. In this safe environment, I was finally breaking the veil of secrecy and ending my silence—and there was no judgment. Talking about abuse was a powerful first step in healing, because I was "unburying" all that pain. Once it was put into the light, it didn't rule me anymore. It didn't "leak out" in explosions of anger or bad decisions. I started to feel capable of ruling myself.

WARRIOR WEEKEND

After attending three ManKind Project meetings, I committed to attend a "Warrior Weekend." These weekend retreats are modeled after a Native American rite of passage initiating boys into manhood—and it was intense. I was pushed physically, but even more so emotionally and psychologically. I was challenged to go beyond the beliefs I'd held about myself as a man. For most of my life, I had believed that I wasn't worthy; I'd operated from a place of fear. But during this weekend, I was pushed to accomplish things I would have never believed possible. I returned from the weekend feeling more powerful, more centered, and more aligned with positive beliefs about myself.

Those weekends aren't for everyone; for some men, the experience is too much. There's no question the experience is tough, because the whole point is to challenge men to reach the potential that's been lying dormant. Although our leaders encouraged us to push through the challenges to get to the personal growth on the other side, they also respected when a man insisted he wanted to be done. Any man was allowed to opt out and leave.

MAKING A COMMITMENT

In my case, my decision to stick with ManKind may have literally saved my life. One of the components of our group meetings involved making a commitment. If it was clear that you were doing something destructive, then you'd commit to making a change, such as to stop drinking, start paying down debt, or stop cheating on your wife.

I had to make a commitment to not commit suicide.

Here's why: shortly after I'd gotten plugged into a ManKind group, I was sued, and later investigated by the FBI. As the lawsuit dragged on and I realized all our savings were going to evaporate, I got to the lowest point I'd ever been. I told the group, "I don't know that I can do this. I'm ready to just be done."

Two of my mentors said, "Rick, we want an ironclad commitment that you will not commit suicide." We talked about that commitment as a group and finally arrived at an agreement I knew I could keep. I agreed to call one of them if I was seriously considering killing myself and not do anything until we talked. Some of the men committed to checking in with me to offer support.

When thoughts of suicide came up, I remembered my commitment. Knowing that I would need to call one of my support guys—who, I knew, would probably talk me out of it—kept me from ever seriously making plans to end my life. I'm not sure what would have happened to me if I hadn't found the group when I did.

Experiencing such honest, safe sharing alongside other men showed me that *healing was possible*. I can't express how powerful that was for me. Through sharing all the pain and negativity that I'd held inside, the demons started to lose their power. I was able to release them, and I started to fill that darkness with light, love, kindness, and compassion.

RESILIENT PEOPLE

I decided I wanted more of that—more love and compassion in every part of my life. I would pass someone on the street and send them love. I might walk near someone who seemed ill or was walking badly and send them love. One day, I helped an elderly woman cross the street and told her, "It's always a privilege to walk alongside a beautiful woman!" She loved that. I don't know whether mentally sending love and kindness to others helped them, but it definitely helped me. Compassion and love started existing in the forefront of my mind.

I wanted to take it further and decided to try to help others heal from abuse. That's when I began doing speaking engagements. I went to see the senior minister at a church I attended in Spring, Texas, and told him, "Jesse, I'm doing this work on abuse, and I'd like to speak."

He said, "Okay, Rick. I'll put you on a Wednesday night."

I asked, "That's it?"

He said, "That's it."

I was terrible. My speech was unpracticed and unfocused. I lost control of the room. I was sure they would never want me back and that this was the end of my speaking career. In spite of that, I got a lot of good feedback. Amazingly, they even invited me back.

After that, I approached the minister at a larger church in the area. He agreed to let me speak, and the church printed out brochures with my picture. This was big-time!

I practiced every night for about three weeks leading up to the event. On the day of the speech, the pastor had me give a three-minute "cameo" at each church service, inviting people to attend my presentation.

I started the three minutes by sharing statistical information about the impact of abuse. I pointed out that its damage is far-reaching and how it destroys trust and perverts love. Then I shared what I, myself, had been learning: "What I know is that you can heal. I won't promise it will be easy, and I won't promise it will happen immediately. But if you make the choice, I promise you will heal and can live a joyful, productive, and happy life." I concluded the cameo by saying, "On behalf of the 7.4 million kids who will probably be abused this year, out of which four will die every day, I invite you to this presentation."

About one hundred people showed up, and the practice paid off: I was good.

As more opportunities to speak came up, I created my nonprofit. It has the same name as this book: Resilient People. The dictionary defines "resilient" as "the ability to recover quickly."[4] When you stretch a rubber band, it comes back: that's resilient. Try to deform something,

---

4   Oxford Dictionaries, s.v. "resilient," accessed September 18, 2018, https://en.oxforddictionaries.com/definition/resilient.

and it will return to its shape: that's resilient. "Resilient," to me, means that each one of us possesses the power to overcome anything.

WORKSHOPS FOR HEALING

Eventually, it became clear that I could provide people with even more help if I offered a workshop along with my story. I worked with Chance Taureau, a mentor from ManKind Project, and Dr. Rosana Scearce, a therapist, to develop a workshop curriculum. The workshop guides participants through several experiences that aim to bring awareness and clarity to the issue of abuse. It ends with an opportunity for people to write a letter about abuse, then verbally share it; our goal is to open the door for participants to go forward in their own healing journey. We establish some of the same basic rules that I found to be so helpful with ManKind Project, like confidentiality and respecting speakers by not interrupting. The workshops end by giving participants the opportunity to burn the letters. Seeing the letters, which often describe such painful experiences, go up in flames provides a release for people.

The workshops were first held in faith communities, such as the churches where I'd first spoken. Then I started speaking at schools as well. At one school event, some of the students raised their hands and asked, "Who should we talk to about this, if we need help?"

I responded, "It seems like you've got a supportive teacher right here. He wouldn't have invited me to speak to you if he didn't understand that abuse is a problem and want to help his students heal." I found out later that one of the students approached his teacher after the workshop and asked to talk about some of the painful experiences in his past. It was incredibly meaningful to me to know that I had helped this young person start to deal with the abuse in his life and begin his journey of healing decades earlier than I had.

Resilient People's mission is exactly that: to help people heal from child abuse. I never believed I would heal. I believed it was my "lot in life" to carry the pain of abuse, and no one ever told me otherwise. I'm now guided by these words by Wentworth Miller: "Let me be to someone else what no one was to me."[5]

I was able to heal, and *you can too*. Don't wait fifty years, like I did, to start your healing journey. I'm incredibly happy where I'm at now, but I wish I had started pursuing healing in my twenties or thirties. It's my hope that my readers will hear this message and start living a joyful, productive life, sooner rather than later!

---

[5] "Wentworth Miller Speech at HRC Dinner (complete transcript)," Maps of the Heart, May 22, 2014, https://mapsoftheheart.wordpress.com/2013/09/12/wentworth-miller-speech-at-hrc-dinner-full-transcript/.

THE MESSAGE FOR ALL RESILIENT PEOPLE

In my lowest days, when I was struggling with thoughts of suicide, I remember driving down a highway. I was deeply depressed about the stressful circumstances in my life and struggling to maintain hope. I looked over and saw a giant semitruck. On the bumper, there was a sticker that said, "It will be all right." When I looked again, the truck was gone.

I couldn't stop thinking about that: "It will be all right." I believe that was an angel. Something beautiful put that out for me when I was in the depths of a depression.

I'm now able to share my story to help others, when—for years—I'd barely been able to acknowledge it myself. In fact, I have a personal motto: "I will never again be ashamed about what happened to me or my desire to tell this story to help others." Shame no longer rules my decisions. Pain no longer calls the shots. I'm free. I've healed.

Having gone from considering suicide to now living with joy, I want to tell you: something beautiful is waiting for you too.

Part II

The Healing Trajectory

CHAPTER FOUR

Becoming Aware of the Signs of Abuse

Here's what I won't tell you: "Follow these seven steps and you will be healed." No person's healing process is the same. There are no "X" number of steps to healing from abuse; a complex journey can't be made that simple. However, there are certain phases that often characterize a journey from abuse towards healing.

THE HEALING TRAJECTORY

The organization Adult Survivors of Child Abuse (ASCA) identifies three general phases of the healing journey:

Remembering, Mourning, and Healing.[1] I prefer to think of those phases as Awareness, Understanding, and Recovery. Regardless of what words you use, these phases outline a trajectory that often occurs.

You can think of these phases as a map to help you move forward in your healing journey. The route you take and the scenery you discover will be unique to you, but knowing these phases may help you plot a route to your desired destination. One thing I will tell you: your healing trajectory can begin the moment you decide you want to be healed.

REMEMBERING/AWARENESS

If you want to heal, you first have to recognize that the abuse happened. For me and others, that's no easy thing; this stage is often said to be the most difficult. Memories of abuse may be driven deep into the subconscious mind, and it's going to take time and work to bring those wounds into conscious awareness. Until they are, a person may experience repeated failed relationships, addictions, or other destructive patterns of behavior, like I did.

So what forces us awake? Often, we have to be triggered

---

[1] This information and the following tables are from *Online Survivor to Thriver Manual*, 4th ed. (San Francisco: The Morris Center for Healing from Childhood Abuse, 2007), http://www.ascasupport.org/_html_manuals/survivortothriver/indexSurvivorManual.html.

by a "rock-bottom" experience before we're ready to face the pain in our past. The ASCA calls this "a breakthrough crisis," which is a helpful way of thinking about it: yes, it's a crisis—but it's going to help lead you to a breakthrough. That crisis might be going to jail, or getting divorced, or suffering a financial failure. Abuse survivors may require a significant wake-up call before they're ready to figure out why they keep sabotaging themselves. At that point, a person might be willing to dig up some of the buried memories.

As I've said, I believe each person's journey to healing will be unique, but I also know it can be helpful to have specific guidelines to mark the path forward. With that in mind, I've listed the key experiences that define the "Remembering" phase, according to the ASCA. If these are helpful, take them to heart. If they're not, leave them alone.

STAGE ONE: REMEMBERING

- I am in a breakthrough crisis, having gained some sense of my abuse.
- I have determined that I was physically, sexually, or emotionally abused as a child.
- I have made a commitment to recovery from my childhood abuse.
- I shall reexperience each set of memories as they surface in my mind.
- I accept that I was powerless over my abusers' actions, which holds *them* responsible.
- I can respect my shame and anger as a consequence of my abuse but shall try not to turn it against myself or others.
- I can sense my inner child, whose efforts to survive now can be appreciated.

I appreciate how much emphasis the ASCA puts on committing to heal and acknowledging that the abuse happened. You can't heal if you keep running from the pain; you have to make the choice to face it. How you do so is up to you, and what comes next will be unique for everyone. But you've got to start with making yourself aware that it happened. Once you can acknowledge your experience of abuse to yourself and someone else, then healing can begin.

MOURNING/UNDERSTANDING

Maybe you've finally become aware of the abuse in your past, or maybe you've always known it was there. It's possible that your memories of abuse have always been right in the forefront of your mind. The next phase abuse survivors usually experience in a healing trajectory is understanding. You acknowledge that it happened, then take steps to understand the knowledge of the abuse and the ways it impacts you now.

Imagine a female college student got drunk at a party and then was sexually assaulted. There will be layers of that experience that she'll need to try to understand. She may struggle with numerous questions about even her own actions: "Why did I go to the party? Why did I drink? Was that stupid? Am I to blame?"

The short answer to that last question is always *No*. Anything other than consensual sex between two fully aware adults is assault, and the victim is never to blame in a case of sexual abuse. It was not your fault! However, it often takes a long time for an abuse survivor to understand this. A survivor may need help from a therapist or mentor to work through the complex feelings associated with abuse.

She'll also need to sort through her emotions about the perpetrators. She might be feeling anger, fear, desire for justice, or any number of emotions. What was her experience after the assault? Did she conceal it? How did that affect her relationships? Did she try to report it? How did people respond? Was she made to feel victimized again? All of these complications need to be sorted through before the survivor reaches a freeing level of understanding.

Sometimes we just need to acknowledge that *something* happened. An experience of abuse may be so deeply painful that a survivor needs to keep it at arm's length. As I shared earlier, the memory from my childhood when Bob took me to his neighbor's house remains dark for me. I have no idea what happened next; I suspect my mind doesn't want me to know. I've gained a lot of understanding about much of the sexual abuse I've experienced, and so I'm content to let that particular memory remain dark. I know *something* happened; that's enough.

This second phase of healing involves more than just understanding the knowledge about the abuse itself; it also involves understanding how the abuse continues to affect you. The ASCA calls this stage "Mourning" because there's tremendous sadness in recognizing all the aspects of life that were stolen from you by abuse. For instance, I was robbed of all the normal sexual development I should have gone through as a teenager; for decades, I couldn't have a healthy sexual relationship with a woman. I also struggled with shame and self-sabotage well into adulthood because of the buried pain from abuse.

When I was in ManKind Project, I had the opportunity to start taking a hard look at some of those unhealthy habits, such as my anger, my drinking, and my pattern of bad decision-making. In ManKind, we talk about the "shadow side"—that's how we discuss the behaviors that aren't working. No one likes talking about their shadow side; it's the part of our personality that we wish wasn't there at all, and sometimes we hide it, even from ourselves.[2] The ASCA has helpful statements about some of the ways we have to wake up to this shadow side. Again, I think it's too simple to say a "seven-step process" will work for everyone, but I can say that the statements below were all part of my own journey.

---

[2] "Frequently Asked Questions," ManKind Project, accessed September 27, 2018, https://mankindproject.org/frequently-asked-questions/#shadow.

> **STAGE TWO: MOURNING**
>
> - I have made an inventory of the problem areas in my adult life.
> - I have identified the parts of myself connected to self-sabotage.
> - I can control my anger and find healthy outlets for my aggression.
> - I can identify faulty beliefs and distorted perceptions in myself and others.
> - I am facing my shame and developing self-compassion.
> - I accept that I have the right to be who I want to be and live the way I want to live.
> - I am able to grieve my childhood and mourn the loss of those who failed me.

Facing the trauma and pain is not easy. However, acknowledging what happened and pursuing understanding is an important phase most people need to experience in the healing trajectory.

HEALING/RECOVERY

The third phase in the healing trajectory is exactly that: Healing! You won't get there by making the mistake I did for so long—you can't look *outside* of yourself to be healed. You have to look *inside* to be healed. It's a challenging thing to do, but on the other side of the long journey, you will be free. You can live a joyful, productive, fulfilling life. You will no longer be burdened by the negative thoughts that hold you back. You can embrace each day and expect good to flow your way, rather than bad.

You will also be a more compassionate, loving human being. Getting through the second phase of understanding will enable you to deal with your "shadow side" and start to strengthen the healthy parts of your life. Your relationships will be stronger, and you will feel fully known.

Read these statements from the ASCA about what healing can look like in this third phase. These sentences describe profound liberty and beauty. I can relate to each of these statements—*this* is the kind of freedom that awaits you on the other side of facing your pain.

> **STAGE THREE: HEALING**
>
> - I am entitled to take the initiative to share in life's riches.
> - I am strengthening the healthy parts of myself, adding to my self-esteem.
> - I can make necessary changes in my behavior and relationships at home and work.
> - I have resolved the abuse with my offenders to the extent that is acceptable to me.
> - I hold my own meaning about the abuse that releases me from the legacy of the past.
> - I see myself as a thriver in all aspects of life—love, work, parenting, and play.
> - I am resolved in the reunion of my new self and my eternal soul.

What an incredibly beautiful experience to be living out that healed reality. However, if you're going to make it through all the challenges to true healing, there are some key considerations to keep in mind.

REQUIREMENTS FOR THE HEALING PROCESS

The Awareness and Understanding phases can get shut down in a heartbeat. It's terrifying to know what happened. We're afraid we might find out we did something wrong or discover something horrible. Quite frankly, you probably will discover something horrible. Abuse is horrible! The healing trajectory is challenging because it involves bringing up repressed memories that were repressed for a reason: that was how we survived as children.

Some people start this road to healing but then run away. We get the bottle. We get the drugs. We get the illicit relationships. The temporary pain of the healing process feels greater than the risks we're taking—worse than the pain of being caught, or put in jail, or hurting the ones we love.

In my own healing process, there were many times I wanted to bail out. My attitude was "Screw this. I'm going to keep drinking and numbing. I've made it this far." But you know what? It wasn't a great life. That's why a *commitment* to healing is important. You need to commit to seeing the journey through.

A violinist who wants to become a world-class musician needs to commit to practicing. A doctor is committed to developing his craft. An athlete is committed to honing her skills. In order to be successful, we all have to commit to doing the hard work. The journey towards healing is no different. If you want to be successful in your healing, you must make a personal commitment to seeing the journey through.

Yes, the healing trajectory is difficult. But I want to make you a promise: if you were abused—no matter what happened, no matter how horrific—I want you to know you can heal. You can live a fabulous, productive, joyful life and fulfill your dreams. This is a journey you're going to go through, and you *can* do it. I did it. Others have done it. You can do it too.

COMMUNITY IS KEY

If and when you hit a wall in your healing, you may conclude that you just can't go any further. That's where empathy, support, and love from others is crucial. Encouraging voices around you—especially from those that have been through a similar process—will tell you that you *are* doing it. When you've hit a painful point, they'll remind you that you can move through the pain. Beyond that, there will be joy.

If you can find loving and empathetic people to coach you through the process, you will come to understand that the experience of abuse was not your fault. You did nothing wrong. It's the caregiver's responsibility to protect the child, no matter what.

My group with ManKind Project made me realize I wasn't alone. For so long, I had tried to look and act normal, believing all the time that I was the opposite of normal.

I'd never talked about my experience with abuse, and so I had no idea abuse was so prevalent in our society. In ManKind, I listened to other men's stories of abuse and saw them listen to my story with understanding. Suddenly, I wasn't isolated anymore. I can't say how powerful that was, to realize I *wasn't alone.*

At the end of ManKind meetings, we get up and hug each other. We put our hands on each other's chest, look each other in the eye, and say, "Love ya, brother." I went through life not feeling love. My adolescent "education"—if you can call it that—taught me that sex was love, so all I looked for was sex. I didn't look for intimacy, or caring, or concern. Part of what makes my life so rich now is being in a truly loving community and sharing a tender, intimate relationship with my spouse.

That empathetic community also helped me go deeper with my healing. The community I found at ManKind meetings held me accountable to the goals and commitments I'd made. When I broke a commitment, they would ask me, "So what was more important than the agreement?" We'd explore that. What was the impact of that decision, on me, on my loved ones? That was a challenging but loving process. Sometimes I would have to say, "Guys, I can't do any more tonight. I'm exhausted." There was no criticism in those moments—but I still had to return to the work the following week. These friends were determined to see me through the low points until I was living a full and productive life. They cared that much about me and my healing.

There's wonder and beauty in a community of people committed to healing. It's magic. However, don't be discouraged if you don't find this empathetic community right away. It took me years before I met Beulah Clay Edmonds or my friends at ManKind Project. It also may take you some time to find a safe, empathetic community—but keep looking until you find it. It's critical to find the *right* place to share your story.

Abuse survivors are often vulnerable. They can easily be taken advantage of by an unhealthy therapist or a toxic community. That's why it's critical to pursue healing in the right place, with the right people. You need to find an empathetic environment, preferably with leaders who are trained in counseling survivors of abuse. I'll talk more about this in chapter 6.

SURRENDER TO THE UNKNOWN

When you begin this process, there's an unknown; you're not exactly sure what happened or what you'll find. Moving forward into that unknown can be frightening. Abuse survivors have spent most of their lives trying to control. We controlled our emotions, we controlled our thoughts—we tried to control everything. That's how we stayed alive.

Unfortunately, those habits of control also left a lot of us messed up. We repressed, buried, self-sabotaged, and brought dysfunction into our relationships. Healing requires *letting go* of some of those bad habits, so that we can replace them with healthy choices and positive truths. There's a surrender involved.

For me, that meant surrendering to a higher power. For others, that simply means you surrender to the process. If you choose to work with a therapist or a group like ManKind Project, you will have to make the choice to follow their recommended process towards healing. In ManKind, that meant agreeing to confidentiality, going on the Warrior Weekend, allowing the other men to check in with me and hold me accountable, and showing up to meetings. Twelve-step programs also have their own process.

Once you find a safe, empathetic environment where you can pursue healing, let your walls come down. Allow yourself to move towards the unknown. Surrender control, so that you can heal and ultimately live a joyful life.

REPRESSION: A BARRIER TO HEALING

For so long, I couldn't even begin my healing journey because I didn't want to acknowledge the abuse in my past. I used a powerful tool to keep all those memories at bay: repression.

Abuse survivors use repression as a protective mechanism. The mind defends us by burying traumatic memories because they feel too painful to deal with and understand. However, as we've discussed, those memories leak out in other ways. Bruce W. Cameron, a licensed professional counselor and psychologist, wrote, "These unresolved memories can stifle [your] growth and development [and lead] to a 'stunted' adulthood in terms of self-esteem and personal identity."[3]

Men may struggle with repression even more than women because of the cultural messages we receive. We're told, "Men don't cry. Toughen up and deal with it. Be a man." That message is harmful; it tells us not to feel. That message ends up producing a lot of insensitive, angry, pain-filled men. Like Bruce W. Cameron says, they're "stunted" adults.

Repression starts with actively trying to *not remember*. I

---

[3] Carolyn Steber, "Signs You Might Be Repressing Negative Childhood Memories," *Bustle*, April 20, 2017, https://www.bustle.com/p/11-signs-you-might-be-repressing-negative-childhood-memories-51958.

tried to help that process along by drinking, doing drugs, and taking stupid risks. I wanted to deaden the painful memories. There's a problem with that, though. As we repress memories, we also repress the feelings that went along with them. Researcher Brené Brown explains the problem this creates: "We cannot selectively numb emotions. When we numb the painful emotions, we also numb the positive emotions."[4] When you deaden your feelings, you deaden them all.

Part of healing requires "resurrecting" those deadened emotions, so you can once again feel joy, gratitude, empathy, and all the other positive emotions you stopped feeling a long time ago. You need to confront those repressed memories and allow yourself to feel the painful emotions connected to them.

The experience may not be pretty. When I first started speaking about my history of abuse, I was like a babbling idiot. I did it in many inappropriate places, and I'd start openly weeping at a party or out in public. It drove my wife, Ann, nuts. I was a mess, but I was learning how to feel again—and that was a good thing. I am now capable of feeling empathy for others. I care about myself; I even love myself.

---

4   Brené Brown, *The Gifts of Imperfection: Let Go of Who You Think You're Supposed to Be and Embrace Who You Are* (Center City, MN: Hazelden, 2010).

There's a piece of advice that we share at ManKind Project: "Be greedy when you seek help. Get all the help you can." When I'm "greedy" about seeking out love and joy, then I've got a whole lot more love and joy to give.

Repression may feel a lot tidier, but it's like being in jail; it holds you in bondage. As a child, repression served you. You were powerless to stop the pain of abuse, and repression was a tool you used for your protection and survival. As an adult, repression no longer serves you; it actually holds you back from real healing.

SIGNS OF REPRESSION

You might be thinking, *One problem though. If I've repressed memories, and the whole point of repression is to hide the memories from my conscious self—how would I know I'm repressing them?* Carolyn Steber, writer for *Bustle* magazine, lists key signs you might be carrying repressed memories of trauma:

- You have strong reactions to certain people.
- Specific places or situations freak you out.
- It's difficult for you to control your emotions.
- Keeping a job has always been difficult.
- You've always struggled with fears of abandonment.
- Friends often say you're "acting like a child."
- You have a tendency to self-sabotage.

- Friends have called you "impulsive" on more than one occasion.
- You often feel emotionally exhausted.
- You always feel anxious.
- You seem to have issues with anger management.[5]

Many of those symptoms described me, before I started dealing with my past. Perhaps they describe you. Let's look at several of those symptoms in greater depth.

Self-Defeating Behavior

Many abuse victims report a pattern of self-sabotage. After I'd quit drinking and start to feel good about it, I would decide my good behavior was worth a celebration. Do you know what I'd do to celebrate? I'd have a drink.

My self-sabotage affected my relationships, too, like my high-school sweetheart and the girl I later got engaged to. When each relationship started getting close to real intimacy, I got terrified and I bailed. I was inconsiderate and cruel to them—the kind of "stunted" adult described earlier, who doesn't know how to feel or show empathy to others.

---

[5] Carolyn Steber, "Signs You Might Be Repressing Negative Childhood Memories," *Bustle*, April 20, 2017, https://www.bustle.com/p/11-signs-you-might-be-repressing-negative-childhood-memories-51958.

Self-sabotage showed up in my work as well—even when I was successful. I remember one high-powered job I was offered. It would have been a great opportunity, but I knew the work would expose my stutter—so I turned it down. I always ran when the going got tough.

Other signs of self-sabotage might be divorce, job instability, or business failures. The motivation for these self-defeating behaviors may get back to a deeply held belief that you don't deserve good things. When something beautiful comes along—like a great relationship or an exciting new job—self-sabotage kicks in. Abuse survivors may simply believe they're not worthy.

Negative Coping Mechanisms

There are also plenty of negative coping mechanisms that abuse survivors may turn to. I've already discussed the role that alcohol and drugs played in my efforts to deaden the pain; those are common negative coping mechanisms. Abuse survivors can also struggle with incredible anger. My anger was explosive and often disproportionate to whatever had set me off.

Isolation is big too. Abuse survivors may have few friends or minimal social contacts—but isolation can occur within relationships as well, especially when you're feeling insecure. Whenever Ann and I had an argument during the first stretch of our marriage, I would isolate myself for weeks, both physically and emotionally. Self-harm, such as cutting, can also be a sign of repressed trauma. For some reason, causing outer pain may seem like a good way to address inner pain; it also can function as a cry for help.

Lack of Boundaries

As an adult, I came to find out that my best friend was cheating on his wife. I had been the best man in his wedding, and I gave him a hard time about his affairs. He continued his extramarital relationships, though, flying his mistress out to be with him. At the time, I was traveling a lot, and my friend asked if he could use my house to meet with this woman. I pushed back, but he kept insisting. Finally, I allowed it. I knew I shouldn't have; I didn't want to—but I did.

Eventually, his wife found out about the affair. She asked her husband, "Where was all this happening?"

He answered, "Rick's house."

They ended up saving their marriage, but my friend's wife didn't want him to be in contact with me anymore. I lost the friendship, something I regret to this day. I could have said, "No, I'm not going to let you use my house.

I'm going to honor your marriage. I can't stop you from having an affair, but I certainly don't have to help you." But I *did* help him cheat on his wife. Why didn't I have the power to tell him no? Why couldn't I draw that moral boundary and stick to it?

A lack of boundaries can be a subtler long-term consequence of abuse. The Heal for Life foundation explains why this would be: "Violent acts of assault or trauma, and extended periods of emotional or sexual abuse, have significant enduring negative effects on the development of boundaries. Children who have been abused often are not allowed...or are never given the chance, to learn their boundaries...They learn that their bodies are not their own. Their boundaries are variable or non-existent."[6]

Learning to create boundaries is part of the normal development of a child; they learn how to identify what to accept or reject: "No, you can't slap me; no, you can't pinch my butt." Typically, a child learns these boundaries from their parents or at school, and they develop a healthy sense of self-respect. That self-respect helps them create boundaries, not just physically, but also morally.

Abused children don't have that. They lose the ability to recognize that they have a sacred space around them, a

---

[6] "The Effect of Trauma on Boundary Development," Heal for Life, August 11, 2013, https://www.healforlife.com.au/the-effect-of-trauma-on-boundary-development/.

space that is theirs—because abuse shattered that sacred space. That boundary is broken, and a victim of abuse no longer understands how to create or defend future boundaries. They come to accept that other people control what happens to them.

Linda Pittman is a survivor of physical and sexual abuse, and gives a firsthand account of dealing with broken boundaries:

> As a child, I could not defend myself against abuse from a bigger and stronger adult. If I tried to defend myself, I was punished more or overpowered. So I learned to submit in hopes that it would be less painful. My physical boundaries were breached over and over. My submission was a coping mechanism to help me through each act of abuse. I learned to allow others to do what they wanted and began to believe that I had no rights over my body. My mental and spiritual boundaries were also breached because the shame of my abuser was transferred to me ("I was bad"), and I was not being "good" as defined by my church.[7]

In Linda's case, the sexual abuse she experienced caused her to feel confusion about her mental and spiritual boundaries as well. Abused children easily lose any con-

---

[7] Linda Pittman, "Rebuilding My Boundaries After Abuse," Overcoming Sexual Abuse, April 2011, https://overcomingsexualabuse.com/2011/04/16/rebuilding-my-boundaries-after-abuse/.

cept of what is moral or right. As they grow up, these missing boundaries can show up in a number of ways. Maybe there's tolerance of degrading sexual innuendos at work. Maybe an abuse survivor is pressured to do things in a relationship that she doesn't want to do but submits to doing anyway. In my work, I often played with the gray line; I made decisions that I knew were wrong because I felt pressure from other people.

The list below identifies common experiences among people who lack good boundaries as a result of abuse. Does this sound like you?

- It is difficult for you to ask for what you want and need, and hard to say "No" to others when you would like to.
- It is easier to take care of other people's needs and desires than your own. It is also easier to go along with them than express your own opinions.
- Other people seem to know you better than you know yourself. They also seem to know what is best for you.
- It is hard to make decisions because you frequently don't know how you are feeling or what you think about important things.
- When feelings are present, they are so strong that they are overwhelming. It is difficult to control the "volume," to turn feelings up or down and still be in touch with them.
- Relationships seem to be one-way, and you always put

more into them than you get out of them. But even though you're not getting what you want, you stay with them just the same.
- Other people's moods have a big effect on you because you feel responsible for them. When they are happy, you are happy. When they are sad or angry, you blame yourself!
- Disturbing thoughts or memories keep popping into your awareness and sensations occur in parts of your body for no apparent reason.
- Concentrating and paying attention are often difficult. You are too easily distracted or influenced by things going on around you.
- Learning from your own mistakes is not easy. You seem to keep making the same errors in judgment repeatedly, and you have little confidence in your own experience.
- Other people seem to have a better grasp on reality than you do, so you depend on them to tell you what is true and real.
- People can take or borrow things from you without returning them or repaying you. What's theirs is theirs and what's yours is theirs.[8]

If you struggle with many of the statements above, that could be a sign that you're experiencing some long-term

---

8   Joel Friedman and Marcia Mobilia Boumil, *Betrayal of Trust: Sex and Power in Professional Relationships* (Westport, CT: Praeger, 1995).

effects of abuse. Creating healthy boundaries is part of the healing that can come once you start facing the abuse in your past.

THE INNER CHILD'S ROLE IN THE HEALING PROCESS

One of my first experiences of therapy was doing transactional analysis, which says that we tend to relate to people as one of three "types": the parent, the child, or the adult. We would often talk about our relationships and interactions in those terms.

For example, if I was letting someone else call the shots and break my boundaries, I was acting more like the child. Sometimes I would overcorrect by lashing out in anger and trying to dominate a situation, like a parent might. The goal was usually to try to act more like an adult: consider all the information and make a mature, balanced choice that was less reactive and more thoughtful.

The child role can go one of two ways: the child can be free, uninhibited, and creative, or the child might adapt to what other people want him to do and submit to their desires. Likewise, the parent role can be either nurturing or dominating. Ideally, a healthy adult can embrace either type, whenever the situation calls for it. If you come across a swimming hole in a remote location, you can be free like the child and go skinny-dipping. If you see a frail woman struggling to lift her groceries, you can be nurturing like the parent and help her out.

The problem is, childhood sexual abuse gets this all messed up. Adult survivors of abuse carry around a traumatized child self, and it causes them to cope in unhealthy ways. They try to handle adult situations with a child's perspective. For instance, consider what we just discussed about boundaries. An abused child who had her boundaries shattered doesn't know how to create space for herself as an adult. She might resort to unhealthy coping mechanisms to get that space. Maybe she lashes out at people in anger or maintains an aloof attitude and never connects with anyone.

Usually, the "child" self is the one to help us be vulnerable. It's the uninhibited persona that is free to take risks—something crucial if we want to connect with other people. But a traumatized inner child is scared to death of that risk. If we hope to experience real intimacy with another person, it's important to heal the inner child.

I literally had to talk to my inner child in order to experience healing in this area. After my ManKind mentors began educating me about healing the inner child, I got a stuffed monkey that I named Chunky. I would talk to Chunky about everything my inner child, Freddy, was scared about. "Okay, Freddy," I'd say, holding Chunky on my lap. "I know this happened. It was horrible. But you did nothing wrong. I will never, ever let that happen again, because I am an adult now. I will protect you." That inner child had to trust that I, as an adult, would be able to protect myself in the future. I needed to counsel that traumatized child before I was able to be vulnerable with other people.

Sound strange? Here's the thing: most of us are having these conversations with an inner child all the time already, subconsciously. Our reactions, our coping mechanisms—a ton of those are filtered through and affected by our traumatized inner child. If you can actually verbalize a conversation with your child self, then you're able to start becoming aware of what's already happening.

Here's another way of explaining it, from Pandora's Project:

> Some Childhood Sexual Abuse (CSA) survivors may have the feeling that their abused child self was someone else, not themselves at a younger age...Acknowledging that you are the adult version of this child who experienced the abuse can be crazy. You did go through the abuse as a child and you survived. Reconnecting with, forgiving, and healing the hurt inner child can be an important part of healing from childhood sexual abuse.[9]

---

9 Melinda, "Healing Your Inner Child after Sexual Abuse," Pandora's Project, accessed October 3, 2018, https://pandys.org/articles/innerchild.html.

Some of the recommendations in that same article talk about reconnecting with your inner child, learning to forgive and "parent" the inner child, and allowing yourself to be a kid again at times.

Working to heal a traumatized inner child can get confusing and might even feel dangerous at times. It's important to do this work in a supportive, therapeutic setting, with people who have experience in this area. Here's why it's worth the trouble: by choosing to gain awareness about your inner child and bring it into your consciousness, you can make different choices. You can make *better* choices.

COMMIT TO HEAL

Repression, self-sabotage, boundary issues, the inner child—there's a lot to get through. It took me decades. But when I made a commitment to heal, the Universe seemed to work with me to help support that healing.

Resilience means you claim the truth that you *can* heal and you *will* heal. You may not know how long it's going to take or how it's all going to work, but you have faith that it will happen.

Yes, it *will* happen!

CHAPTER FIVE

My Story Continues: Waking Up to Self-Defeating Patterns

I'd worked hard. There had been countless late nights and weekend stints at the office until I'd finally managed to get the company out of its huge financial mess. Finally, the business started running smoothly and turning a profit. I felt pretty good about that. When anybody needed anything, I got it; if the president needed something, I delivered. My position felt powerful and necessary.

It felt only fair that I enjoy the fruits of my labor, so I started taking longer lunches. I'd have a drink with lunch, maybe two, maybe more. Sometimes I came in a little late, a little hungover.

GETTING PAST DENIAL

A close friend of mine, the assistant controller, was often in a position where she needed to cover for me. Sometimes I had a bad attitude that she had to explain away; sometimes I neglected to get important tasks done, and she wound up doing them for me. I think she got tired of it.

She could also see what I couldn't see about myself: I was in bad shape.

This woman came in one day and said, "I need to talk to you." She closed the door and sat down. "Rick," she said, "you've done a lot for my career. I don't have a degree. I would have never gotten this job if you hadn't gone to bat for me. But I don't want to cover for you anymore. These long lunches, the drinking—I'm done trying to cover that up. You need help," she told me. "You need to get your life fixed."

In retrospect, I think it took a lot of guts for her to tell me that, but in the moment, I felt all kinds of righteous indignation. *After all I've done for her*, I thought. So I did what I usually did after getting off work: I hit a bar. The first drink was always wonderful. The second drink was good. The third and fourth usually made me unconscious.

The next day at work, my boss called me into his office. He said, "Rick, I need to talk to you."

"Sure!" I said. "Whatever you need, I've got it."

He said, "Rick, you're probably one of the best financial people I've ever worked with. You did a lot to make me look good when I took over this presidency—but you're screwing up. You've got to clean your life up, or I'm going to fire you."

I was stunned. "Anything else?" I asked.

"No," he said.

I called up my best friend and asked him to meet me at a brewery for lunch. When he arrived, I started fuming. "You won't believe this—after all that I've done for this company, all the long days, all the weekends I worked," I ranted, pouring down one drink after another.

My friend looked at me and said, "Rick, I'm probably your best friend."

"You are my best friend," I told him.

"You need help," he told me. "You're out of control. Your life is going the wrong way, and I think you need to get therapy."

They say the Universe taps you on the shoulder. That wasn't enough for me, so then it knocked me on the head. I still didn't listen, so then it hit me with a two-by-four. I think I would have remained in denial for the rest of my life if I hadn't been hit hard with those three accusations in the span of two days—all from people who cared about me.

Finally, I started to listen. At my best friend's recommendation, I started meeting with a husband-and-wife counseling team. My therapy with them helped me deal with the nightmares I'd been having but didn't go so far as to uncover the sexual abuse. Still, the dreams stopped, and I at least made attempts to stop drinking. I felt good—I thought, "Yeah, I've got this." But I was still nowhere near healed.

So, the Universe ran me over with a dump truck.

In 2011, I got into a business transaction that turned into a four-year legal battle. I was accused of securities fraud and investigated by the Securities and Exchange Commission. To get the lawsuit settled, I ended up having to drain every last dime from our investment account; the fund went from $2 million to zero.

The mess didn't stop there. A colleague whom I had helped and was friends with all my life turned on me. My daughter had warned me about him years ago; she could see ugliness in his character that I couldn't. I didn't listen to her, though. This colleague hired the ex-head of the southern district FBI to investigate me for fraud.

I knew about the investigation and initially thought I could help them. When I got a call from the FBI, I said, "I'm not surprised you called. How can I help you?"

The voice on the other end said, "Mr. Huttner, you need to know before you say anything that you are a target of a criminal investigation." My heart sank. I hired another lawyer, and the long battle continued.

I had been attending my ManKind Project meetings at that point, but as I became suicidal, I started meeting with an additional therapist, Rosana Scearce. During one session, the thoughts I confided made her concerned enough that she asked me to call Ann. "Call your wife," she said, "or I'm going to hospitalize you against your will." Ann was out of town, and Rosana asked her to fly to Houston immediately. Rosana ordered me to stay with a friend of hers all day until Ann arrived. Between the commitment I'd made with my leaders at ManKind and Rosana's vigilance, I was saved from committing suicide.

That was "rock bottom" for me; that was the Universe's dump truck. But that was also the moment when I was genuinely ready to commit to healing. I was finally prepared to do the hard work that would be required, because I couldn't stay a minute longer in the dysfunctional place I was in. I had to deal with my pain or I was going to die.

KNOW THYSELF

At a seminar I attended much earlier in my life, I'd heard a quote that stuck with me. Supposedly, the statement hung over the ancient temple at Delphi where warriors and leaders came to consult with the oracle. The words read, "Know thyself." The point made at the seminar was that it's critical to know both your strengths and weaknesses.

The seminar speaker had said, "We all know our strengths pretty well. It's our weaknesses that will kill us." I was in my sixties when I recollected that advice and realized that I had never really tried to know myself.

For years, I had relied on a veneer as protection. I'd created an image, a false story: "This is who I am, look at me." Or, when I felt afraid, "My head's down. *Don't* look at me."

I remember a woman once calling me out on that veneer. I was in a three-day program, and leaders came around to each participant, telling us what they saw. The woman looked at me and said, "Slick. Deceptive." She was dead-on. I had carefully crafted an image—I wore Armani suits; I looked good; I could sell you anything. But none of that was sincere. I was terrified about what people would think if they really knew me.

I'll be honest: I was terrified about what *I* would think when I really knew me. The temple at Delphi was asking for a lot. But, as I said, when I hit rock bottom, I had to choose to either heal or die.

Another memory surfaced around this same time, from an event that happened when I was in my late thirties. I inadvertently met His Holiness the Dalai Lama on an airplane. He was sitting right behind the first-class bulkhead, along with a number of assistants. I felt incredibly drawn to him. I walked right past the bulkhead and knelt down in front of him. His assistants jumped up—they were all strong, powerful guys—but the Dalai Lama just looked me in the eyes. He extended his hands.

I said, "You are the spiritual leader of your people."

He said, "Yes."

I said, "You've been evicted from your country."

"Yes," he said again.

"Where do you get your strength to continue doing the incredible work you're doing?" I asked.

He responded, "Ah, I don't get it from my friends. My friends don't challenge me; they love me. But my enemies, that's where I learn about myself. When I know my weaknesses, I can then enhance my strengths." He explained he was only able to be strong for his people because he'd listened to what his enemies taught him about his problems and weaknesses. It all came back to self-reflection.

That event took place three decades before I actually began to take his advice—but I remembered it. All along, the Universe had tried to give me messages, and I just hadn't been paying attention. Finally, I was ready to listen.

SELF-EXAMINATION

My meetings with ManKind Project had brought up the idea of the "shadow self" I mentioned in the previous chapter. When we're making "bad" decisions that go against how we consciously want to live, that's when the shadow self is behind the wheel. These conversations in ManKind required a great deal of reflection; if I broke an agreement and made a bad decision, I had to think about what I'd prioritized above my agreement.

This forced me to consider my unconscious motivations.

What was driving me? I came up with an idea to hang a sign in my home office that read, "What am I thinking?" Every time I glanced at the sign, I took an inventory of the thoughts going through my head at that moment.

I was stunned to discover how many negative thoughts I was having—not every day or every hour, but every minute. I dreaded going to the mailbox, for instance, because I expected bad news. I was always afraid when I had to speak, because I stuttered so much. There were constant thoughts of someone dying—Ann or one of the kids. If I had a flight coming up, I would envision the plane crashing. It occurred to me that I was probably attracting *more* negativity to myself because of my constant mental pessimism.

To increase my awareness about these negative thoughts, I began to write them down. For example, if I was in the middle of a business meeting, I might think, *if they really knew me, they wouldn't want to do business with me.* Later when I got home, I'd get quiet, meditate, and invite that thought into my conscious mind. Then I'd write about it. Journaling enabled me to see the words that I would never say, but that I'd always believed. When writing them, I could begin to discover what was really in my subconscious mind. That was powerful.

The journaling was a long process; it usually took several

sessions before I began to understand any given fear. I'd like to tell you there were huge changes that happened every time I sat down to write: journal about it, boom, fears are gone. It wasn't that easy, but I was persistent. I had made the commitment to heal, and I had accountability from good friends helping me along. Without either of those in place, I probably would have backed out of the process and gone to have a drink. But my community of support wouldn't allow that, and I was determined to see the process through.

Before trying to "know myself," I would have normally pushed those negative thoughts away and tried to think about something else, like sex. Those fear-driven thoughts never went away, though; they just got buried. Once buried, they turned into the "demons" I've talked about. Fear, anger, and pain would leak out at the most inappropriate times, and in the most inappropriate ways.

Now, with a determination to know myself, I brought them into the light. I invited the thoughts to surface and allowed myself to feel them. That was usually uncomfortable. Bad thoughts generally produced bad emotions. But in feeling the pain of these negative emotions, I was learning to "un-numb" myself. I started feeling more joy, compassion, and empathy—all the emotions I had deadened. Plus, when I got through experiencing the negative feeling, the fears started to slowly disappear.

A major tipping point for me came when I confronted the negative belief that I was somehow to blame for the childhood abuse I'd suffered. I was convinced that I'd committed this unforgivable sin and was afraid God would punish me. I ended up punishing myself worse than God ever would have.

After a lifetime of blaming myself, I finally realized, *I didn't do anything wrong.* I was a loving, beautiful, innocent child. It was the caregiver's responsibility to protect me, not mine. I did nothing wrong. I wrote those words down and stared at them. *It wasn't my fault.* Later, I spoke the words out loud at ManKind, and new positive beliefs started taking hold.

I started hanging more signs in my office or anywhere else I would see them. One sign, which I hung during my episode of back pain, says, "I'm stronger every day, and I'm stronger in every way." Another sign, which I read every morning and evening, says simply, "God is good." Another one says, "Nothing without joy." I've spent years replacing negative thoughts with positive ones.

There's an old acronym using the letters in the word FEAR: **F**alse **E**xperiences **A**ppearing **R**eal.

For most of my life, I had indulged those fears. I would think of a point of tension with Ann, for instance—let's say about how we spent our money. I'd begin to imagine a future fight with her about it; I'd imagine what she would say and envision my angry responses. I'd carry the fight on in my mind, until it escalated and escalated. Then I'd imagine her leaving me; then I'd imagine divorce. My fears, which felt so vivid in my mind, then turned into a self-fulfilling prophecy. I would work myself up so much that I'd go and pick the fight with Ann in real life.

As I became more aware of my unconscious motivations, I started having more control over my fears. I'd start an argument in my mind, but then stop. I could tell myself, *wait a minute, that hasn't happened. That's a fear I'm creating about the future, and it isn't real.* I learned to monitor my mind and thoughts. Eventually, when a negative thought came in, I could look at it, reject it, and let it drift away. I didn't pull it in.

INCORPORATING LOVE INTO THE HEALING PROCESS

Someone complained to me recently that he didn't have any friends. When I asked him if he was friendly, he admitted that he wasn't. "Start being friendly," I told him. "Begin by being friendly to yourself, and people will view you differently. If you don't have enough love, be loving. Put your love out there somewhere—go to a shelter or an old age home and be loving. Be kind, and kindness will flow into your life."

I had to learn that advice firsthand. Before I began this healing process, I could easily slip into anger, hatred, and revenge. I'd lose myself in those emotions, and they became incredibly real, draining my energy. Until I began healing on the deepest level, I felt no love for myself. It's hard to love when you're constantly feeling anger, hatred, and revenge. I was locked in an abusive mentality where I kept abusing myself. I could be mean to others too. I was never violent, but I could be rude, sarcastic, and verbally demeaning.

I used to wake up and dread the day as soon as I opened my eyes. I'd think, "Shit. What's going to happen today?" I did not expect good, and I did not believe I deserved good. Something had to change. I had to start being kind to myself. I had to start allowing love and positivity in.

One morning, I remembered an old saying from the Bible: "This is the day the Lord has made. Rejoice, and be glad in it." I began saying that every morning, repeating it multiple times if it didn't initially sink in. I started getting out of bed feeling a bit better, feeling less dread. Not long after I started this habit, I went into the bathroom and made eye contact with myself in the mirror. I realized that I never looked at myself in the eyes; I don't think I ever looked in anyone's eyes. I was afraid of the shame or the guilt that they would see.

But that morning, I looked at myself and said, "Good morning, sweetheart. God loves you, and I love you." The words just came to me. That was the first time I'd ever said to myself, "I love you," and a huge smile broke out on my face. Initially, Ann thought it was the silliest thing in the world, but I didn't care. When I started the morning with those words, I couldn't come out of that bathroom without smiling. After all the work in ManKind, all the therapy, all the effort to clear my consciousness of negative thoughts, I had somehow arrived at a place where I could love myself.

Awareness had led to knowing myself. Knowing myself had led me to the realization that I'm a beautiful human being. The truth was that I'd always been a beautiful human being. What a radical difference it made to finally begin to live life with that belief!

NEUROLINGUISTIC PROGRAMMING

In addition to journaling, modifying my thoughts, and surrounding myself with positive messages, I also benefited from something called neurolinguistic programming (NLP).

NLP posits the theory that we process information in three different ways.

One way is called kinesthetic. People who process kinesthetically learn by moving and doing. Kinesthetic is also the mode most attached to *feeling*, and often, when we're feeling deeply, the human tendency is to look down. When I was doing NLP in therapy, I would access the kinesthetic mode by looking down; the predicate from that position would be "I feel."

The second state is auditory. Auditory processors learn best by *hearing*. When trying to put myself in this mode, I would lift my chin, so my eyes were level and I was able to scan back and forth. The predicate in this mode would be "I say."

Finally, there's visual processing, which focuses on what you *see*. The position that best matches with visual is looking up, as though you're looking far off into the distance. I would put myself in this mode by raising my eyes and saying "I see."

This might sound confusing, but let me explain why it ended up being a helpful tool for me. When I began drifting down into negative emotions, like depression, anger, hatred, or revenge, I realized I was often literally looking down at the ground. Maybe I'd be reliving the past, or I'd be creating my future in a negative way—but either way, I'd turn my gaze downward and fall fast down the slippery slope of negativity.

The NLP work made me realize what a difference our literal body position can make. I remembered a phrase from my childhood religious training—which of course I'd hated, although this phrase was helpful—"I lift up mine eyes unto the hills, whence cometh my help. My help cometh from the Lord." I started thinking about that: "I lift up mine eyes." Eventually, I gave it a try.

I think the biblical passage means "I lift my eyes to God." I still don't love using the term "God" or "Lord," but I do like thinking about aligning my thoughts with Divine thoughts. In either case, it worked for me. When I lifted my eyes up, I was put into a different emotional state. When I began to fall down that slippery slope of negative emotions, I'd lift my arm and point up. I'd raise my eyes and say, "I lift mine eyes up unto the hills, whence cometh my help. My help cometh from the Divine."

In doing this, I was recreating my consciousness in a way that allowed in love. I was opening myself up to receive the good things. I believe you can only give others what you embody. If I can't love myself, I can't love you. I can't love anything. Changing my body helped me actually *embody* more positivity.

FIRST THOUGHT / SECOND THOUGHT

I also came up with my own strategy called "first thought

/ second thought." I often realized that my first thoughts were negative. When I first became aware of that, I started judging myself for that negativity—but that just piled on more negative thinking. My self-judgment wasn't at all loving.

I decided I wasn't going to beat myself up for that first thought—after all, I had been reflexively thinking that way my entire life. However, I decided I *would* hold myself responsible for my second thought. After the first thought came in, I made myself aware of it—and then shifted it, changing from a negative first thought to a positive second thought.

For example, if I was having an argument with myself about something Ann did, I might realize that I was putting myself in a fear-based place. Once I became aware of that, I could shift. I might realize, "Wait a minute—this woman loves me. She cares about me." That second thought would break me out of a negative tailspin. It also kept me from creating self-fulfilling prophecies related to my fears. Rather than go out and pick a fight with someone, I could shift my thinking and have a healthy interaction. This strategy had a powerful impact on my mind.

I'm sure my collection of strategies seems strange—but they worked for me. I want people to understand that there's no single way to pursue healing; what worked for me might not work for you, and what ends up working for you may not have been good for me. However, in one form or another, you'll need to begin your process with awareness. Know thyself, and then open yourself to the messages of love that are trying to get your attention.

LAYERS AND DOORS

As I began to heal, I would sometimes conclude, "I'm done"—but I was never done. I'm still not done! There was always more to discover, another layer deeper to go.

Doors to healing continued to open as I sought to expose the core of who I truly was. I made the choice to open those doors and walk through them. I'm still able to learn new truths about myself by examining my thoughts. When a negative thought comes into my head now, I don't run from it—I examine it. I consider whether it's something I want to explore or something I want to let go. The result has been continued discovery, strength, and healing.

I don't know that I'll ever fully forget the abuse I experienced, but it doesn't run me anymore. I don't get into a depression or play the victim; I don't feel sorry for myself. I'm able to recognize that the abuse is part of my story. Ultimately, my journey through it led me closer to the

Divine. I learned to control my own mind and discovered who I truly am: I'm loved and loving, and there is a loving God. My life is a gift, and my gift is to help other people heal.

My hope is that you one day have your own story of healing to share. I hope you make the decision to heal—and commit to seeing it through. Allow yourself to remember what happened. Believe it happened; it is true for you. Break your silence; share your story about what happened, in the right place, with the right people. When you say the words, the pain loses power. Understand it wasn't your fault; *you did nothing wrong as a child*. Grieve, mourn, and get your anger out; confront the abuser if necessary and move on. Get in touch with your hurting inner child and love that child. In doing so, you wind up loving yourself more.[1]

AN ABUNDANCE OF GOOD

For most of my life, I tended to think there was only so much love, only so much kindness, only so much money. I assumed that most of those good things were for others and that there wasn't enough for me. But that's not true—there's an abundance, even an unlimited supply. The only thing that kept me from experiencing it was my mind, my belief system.

---

[1] Paraphrase of work in Laura Davies, *Allies in Healing* (New York: Harper Collins, 1993).

Consider these words from another sign I've hung in my office, words I can't read often enough: "There is a limitless field of good. I expect good to flow to me...I receive good and expect more good to follow. Nothing is too good to be true for me. Better and better good is coming to me every day in every way...There is no limit to the good that is mine. Everywhere I go, I see good. I feel it, I experience it, and I joyfully share it...I'm grateful for all the good that comes to me."[2]

I read that quote for a long time before I fully believed it. I had to *believe* differently to have a different life. Now, I live the life I choose. I recognize that I deserve what is good, and it's enabled me to live with joy.

Perhaps you struggle to believe such words, but this is true for you as well! You can live a life of abundant good, love, robust productivity, and fulfillment. Decide to heal, commit to it, do the work, and see it through.

---

[2] Ernest Holmes, *Living the Science of the Mind* (Marina Del Rey, CA: DeVorss, 2008).

CHAPTER SIX

Finding a Safe Place to Talk and Share

Twitter.

Facebook.

At a cocktail party, while holding bruschetta.

What do these three things have in common? They're all bad places to share your story of abuse for the first time.

I know this firsthand, because I did it. When I first started building my awareness about how abuse had impacted me, I just wanted to talk about it. As I've shared already in this book, I put my wife in some embarrassing situations by opening up about my experience of abuse at social gatherings. While I was tearing up, my friends were muttering, "What is wrong with him?"

Ann kept telling me that I had to pick a place to share other than dinner parties at our friends' houses. Fortunately, I knew these people well, and we're still friends—but none of them were counseling professionals. They didn't know how to handle what I was sharing, and they felt understandably uncomfortable.

Social media can be an even worse place to share your story because you can't control what anyone does with the information you provide—and sometimes, people may choose to be cruel. After you become vulnerable with your most painful memories, you run the risk of peers leaving mean comments or using what you shared against you.

Abuse is painful already, and healing is challenging enough. You don't need mean comments or eye rolls making the process any harder. Brené Brown writes, "If we can share our story with someone who responds with empathy and understanding, shame can't survive. If we share our shame story with the wrong person, they can easily become one more piece of flying debris in an already dangerous storm."[1]

Your story could trigger something fearful in someone else, which could come out as anger leveled against you. It's not safe to deal with those deep, deep emotional issues in an unprofessional setting, because you don't know what you're going to get.

You *should* share your story—that's an important part of the healing process—but choose to share in a setting that is safe and supportive. That might look like a professional setting with a psychologist or a therapist trained in abuse counseling. It could also be in a group therapy environment, like I found with ManKind Project.

DEFEAT SHAME THROUGH SHARING

As discussed earlier, survivors of child abuse usually have shame, which is a result of secrecy, silence, and judgment. The secrecy can start as a result of pressure from the abuser. In my case, Bob told me that he loved me, then said I could never tell anyone about what had happened. He was a big guy, a friend of my parents, and a cop. Never in a million years did I think I could disobey that command: secrecy.

---

[1] Brené Brown, *The Gifts of Imperfection: Let Go of Who You Think You're Supposed to Be and Embrace Who You Are* (Center City, MN: Hazelden, 2010).

An abuse victim might also be pressured by their family to stay silent: "We don't air our dirty laundry. We'll deal with this within the family." As a result, they may live decades carrying secrecy and undeserved shame. This then leads to self-judgment, fear of judgment from others, and other self-defeating problems that can heap on more shame.

Still, you can't heal what you can't acknowledge. Somehow, you have to break the veil of silence. It takes a lot of courage to do that; in my case, it took enormous pain before I could wake up to my need to deal with the abuse. It was the recurring back pain, the failed business ventures, the confrontations from friends, the lawsuits—all of that had to hit before I was ready to be honest about my past. When I finally could admit that there was something seriously wrong with me, I was forced to ask questions and eventually found answers by looking within.

Once abuse survivors are ready to confront their history of abuse, they need to tell the truth. They need to be authentic and real. I struggled to do this; I had lied to myself and everyone else for close to forty years, trying to convince everyone that I was fine. I lied to justify inappropriate behavior; I pretended I didn't have issues with anger or alcohol. I spent so much of my life trying to look perfect, to do the right things, to impress people in business settings and social settings, but all the while, I was scared shitless. Finally, I had to sit down and tell the truth:

I was abused. And not only that, there was a lot in my life that was damaged because of that abuse.

Then you have to *keep* telling the truth. The whole truth probably won't come out the first time. As you peel back layers, you'll keep discovering more. My first "truth-telling" acknowledged the abuse. Then I had to start looking at some of my negative behavior impacted by abuse. I didn't like that—but I was in a supportive environment with other men who helped me look at those bad choices. Once I faced those new hard truths, I could start dealing with my belief systems around those choices and change my behavior.

I had some real ugliness in me. I didn't want to face that, but by not facing it for most of my life, I'd continued to do ugly things, which made the shame grow. Once I began telling the truth about my behavior, I was freed up to believe something new. That was its own journey.

For instance, I had to do a lot of apology writing. I wrote words that spelled out in no uncertain terms the ugliness I'd done. From there, I could own my guilt, do my forgiveness work, bless it, and then move on.

Facing the bad truths also helped me allow in more of the good. I came to recognize that I am a beloved child of a Divine Being. I genuinely like myself, and other people like me. By facing myself honestly, I arrived at a beautiful understanding of my worth and my purpose. I could recognize the truth of what happened to me, *knowing* the abuse occurred through no fault of my own.

I could say this a thousand times: abuse was not your fault, no matter what. You can heal! Start with awareness and acknowledgment. Once you make yourself aware of the abuse, you can begin to understand all the ways it impacts your life.

Sharing your story can play a crucial part in your healing journey; it's by sharing with others that empathy and compassion can take the place of shame. However, it's critically important that you choose a safe place to begin this process.

CONDITIONS OF A SAFE PLACE

As Laura Davis writes in *Allies in Healing*, "When the desire to heal is met with information, skilled support, and a safe environment, survivors grow in ways they never dreamed possible."[2]

One of the first people you share your story with might be a trusted friend, a teacher, or a mentor. These people can do a lot to help you, especially if they listen attentively,

---

[2] Laura Davies, *Allies in Healing* (New York: Harper Collins, 1993).

show you empathy, and keep your story confidential. Ultimately, though, it's going to be important to work with people who are experienced in working with abuse survivors. They can offer you tools, safety, and information that an inexperienced friend simply won't have.

That doesn't mean that all therapy groups are safe places or that all counselors are trained in abuse recovery. You can determine whether a setting is safe or not by paying attention to certain "rules."

Confidentiality: Make sure that the person or people you choose to share your story with will keep your story confidential. In ManKind Project, we call our groups a "container" because of the confidentiality ground rules—you have no authority to share what another man has said, unless you have his permission—and those rules are enforced. That's a good thing; we all know we're safe to be as open as we need to be.

Empathy, not criticism: Share your story with people who will support you, not criticize you. There should be no ridicule, mockery, or judgment. Your goal is to find people who will show empathy and compassion.

I was afraid that when people heard my story, they wouldn't like me anymore. I expected them to evict me from their lives. Yet when I told my story at ManKind

Project, *nothing bad happened to me.* The huge fears that had grown exponentially in my mind while bottled up were spoken out loud—and strangely enough, when I acknowledged them in the company of other listeners, they no longer seemed so threatening. The other men didn't criticize me; they loved me and leaned in. I wasn't alone. This experience gave me the freedom to keep looking deeper within.

Abuse survivors often are hard enough on themselves. You don't need other people being hard on you too; mostly, you need a safe place where you can share your story and receive loving support from your listeners.

No interruptions: In our ManKind groups, there's a rule a man can hold the floor until he says, "I'm done." Even if he pauses for several minutes, the floor remains his until he gives it up. In a space like that, you know you're going to be heard out. There's going to be time to think and contemplate, if you need it. Many times, the deepest, truest stuff would come out after those pauses. The not interrupting rule is useful for healing, but it's also an important way for listeners to show their respect.

Support: Before I found ManKind Project, I flew around the country attending healing seminars and workshops. Many of the seminars provided something helpful, but the "weekend workshop" model didn't enable any long-term growth. I showed up, I did my "shtick," and then I left.

At ManKind Project, I showed up every week for years and committed to sticking with it. I got to know myself better in doing that, but also, I was there long enough that the guys learned to see through the mask I wore. They called me out when they saw I was being dishonest and knew me well enough to help me work through my shadow. If I made an agreement, they held me to it. If I failed to keep it, they helped me discover why, in a loving way. The environment fostered integrity, accountability, and love. That accountability and support helped me in a huge way during the hardest times in my healing journey.

The support came in other ways too. It was helpful to have *trained* leaders, who were knowledgeable about dealing with men experiencing high stress. They knew how to help men express rage in a safe way, and that was often important. We also were provided information and resources when we needed them.

In your healing journey, look for a place that can offer you support with resources and knowledge, in addition to accountability and love.

DO YOUR HOMEWORK

Wherever you decide to pursue healing, check it out thoroughly. If you join a group, attend it for a while and pay attention to how everyone interacts. Listen. When you share, don't share everything at once; wait until you know for sure that the setting is genuinely safe.

If you're going to hire a therapist, interview them. Go online and research good questions to ask. Ask about their experience working with survivors of abuse. What's their history? What are their methods? Have they seen successful healing with their other patients? Listen to your intuition. If it feels wrong, it's probably not a good fit. I'll discuss this more in the next chapter.

SAFE PLACES
ManKind Project

I've already talked extensively about ManKind Project, so it's clear I would recommend their groups. The leaders in ManKind are extensively trained and have to be regularly recertified. Their own integrity is closely examined, so that they can be trusted to lead other men. In my opinion, their model for helping men live into their full potential is excellent.

Woman Within

ManKind Project's counterpart group for women is called Woman Within. They also have ground rules to help establish a safe place for sharing. On their website, they say, "Our woman's empowerment process offers a safe place where you can be held when you feel alone, challenged when you're stuck, and loved when you believe that you aren't worthy. And you can choose to live life to the fullest."[3] Although, as a man, I obviously have not attended any of their meetings, I've heard good things from female friends of mine.

Adult Survivors of Childhood Abuse

Another group I'm familiar with is a nonprofit called Adult Survivors of Childhood Abuse (ASCA). Their meetings, like ManKind Project's, include rules and boundaries; confidentiality is strict, and there are no interruptions allowed. They've also created extensive resources about how to operate an ASCA meeting; people can become self-trained through the material to become group leaders. ASCA's excellent information about the phases of healing has been referenced already in this book.

I attended an ASCA group for a time in Houston and found it quite helpful. The leaders there were mostly

---

3   "Home Page," Woman Within International, accessed October 11, 2018, http://womanwithin.org/.

laypeople who had been abused and desired to create a safe place for others to share. They did a great job modeling commitment and making it safe for people to be open. It's also safe for people to just listen; I attended for months, and one man never said more than hello and goodbye. That was okay. ASCA's leaders aren't professionally trained like the leaders in ManKind, and in my experience the healing "work" didn't go as deep or as far. However, it was a great first step to begin to share my story. Also, whereas ManKind is for any man who wants to become a better person in general, ASCA is more narrowly focused on providing support for abuse survivors.

Resilient People

Then there's Resilient People, my own nonprofit. Our goal is to make abused people aware of abuse, provide information about the healing trajectory of abuse, and help abuse survivors know that they can lead a resilient life—a joyful, productive, happy life. It may not be easy, but it's possible. We deliver our message through speaking engagements and a follow-up workshop. I'm also trying to get that message out through the publication of this book! You can see more at our website: www.resilientpeople.us.

In an appendix at the end of this book, you'll find more organizations that offer support to abuse survivors, along with other books that may be helpful. I haven't personally attended meetings at these other organizations, so it's important to remember to do your research into whether or not you'll encounter a safe place there. Keep in mind the characteristics you want to look for: **confidentiality, empathy, guidance rather than criticism, no interruptions,** and **support**. A *supportive* environment will offer encouragement, provide resources, and should be led by thoroughly trained people.

THE HEALING THAT COMES FROM SHARING

Abuse survivors once had power robbed from us. Our abusers told us we didn't have the right to protect our bodies, so we came to believe we didn't have rights at all. When you share your story, you're able to take some of that power back. Through opening up about my story, I remember feeling newly empowered. I didn't have to keep anyone's secret; it was my right to share my own story. That was energizing and powerful—no wonder I couldn't shut up about it!

Being able to share your story is a crucial part of healing. When others hear your story of abuse and respond with empathy, the demons inside of you that held you back start to lose their power. I decided I wanted to run my own life. I didn't want the abuse to run my life for me. Sharing my story helped me take the reins into my own hands. Although it felt scary to bring up some of the darkest stuff inside of me, the support I found from others helped me bring it up anyway. Fear didn't rule me!

This chapter emphasizes the importance of sharing, but also the importance of *where* to share. Context is critical. Be careful of where you talk. Whether you choose to share your story with a best friend, with a therapist, or in group therapy, make sure you will be safe, supported, and heard. Expect that you might need to try a few places before you find the right fit.

Although many women have shared stories of sexual assault via Twitter and Facebook through the #MeToo movement, I don't recommend you share your story online before you've done some thorough healing work. Words posted online become a public record that never goes away, and there's no way to control what response you get.

Like Brené Brown said, harsh responses can just become more flying debris in an already difficult storm. If you've already shared your story a number of times and have experienced substantial healing from abuse, you'll be in a better place to share your story publicly if you choose. You'll be less vulnerable to criticism at that point and have a better idea about what will be helpful to others.

I used to be terrified of public speaking because of my

stutter, and I lived in fear that people would find out who I truly am. But now, I'm able to speak in front of large groups of people, and I tell them *exactly* who I am. I've even been able to confront Bob, a story that I share later in this book. How did I get there? I was supported in a safe environment when I shared my story in the beginning; because of that, I've healed enough to now share it widely.

Eventually, your story will be just that: a story. It will be a collection of facts from your life that no longer has the power to hurt you, because you will have taken the power back through your healing process.

CHAPTER SEVEN

Locating a Professional Therapist Trained to Treat Abuse Survivors

"Rick, you need help."

"Clean your life up, or I'll fire you."

"Your life is going the wrong way, and I think you need therapy."

In two days, three of the people closest to me made it

crystal clear that they thought I needed professional help. The third person, my best friend, gave me the names of a husband-and-wife therapist team. It was in their company that I had my first experience with professional counselors.

At that point in my life, I was still "slick and deceptive." I'd only begun to realize that I genuinely needed help and was still scared to death of what people would think if they really knew me. I wasn't ready for group therapy; I didn't have the maturity or courage to share my story in front of a group. At that point, I needed the help of a private therapist.

THE ROLE OF ONE-ON-ONE PROFESSIONAL THERAPY

Group therapy and individual therapy can work together beautifully. In a group setting, you realize you're not alone and can receive support from other empathetic individuals. If the group setting is like ManKind Project, you can also participate in practices that will push your healing further, like meditating, making agreements, and being held accountable.

Individual therapy can play an important role too: your healing can move faster than in a group setting where you're sharing the time with many other people. In one-on-one therapy, there's enough space and time to fully explore the areas of your life in need of examination. A trained professional will also have knowledge and strategies for your healing that a layperson leading a group therapy session wouldn't have. Also, one-on-one therapy might feel like the safest place to begin to share your story. It's difficult for a survivor of abuse to say words like "I was raped by my father." Those words might be easier to get out in a private setting with a trained professional than in a larger group context.

It's possible that your story of abuse may be straightforward enough that you could fully heal by simply going to a good group. However, as one doctor told me, multiple traumas can be difficult to work with. Trained therapists have superior skills in dealing with complicated, challenging trauma. When the pain goes deep, is connected to multiple events, and impacts multiple areas of your life, it can be highly beneficial to see a trained professional. It might even be necessary if you hope to fully heal.

When I did individual therapy, I was able to speak in confidence about my issues. I could look at my recurring nightmares and explore the pain behind my drinking—and I felt safe doing so. Finally, my counselors determined I was ready to go into a group. The married couple I worked with helped lead the groups as well, so the groups were well-managed, and I felt safe making the transition. Ironically, a close friend of mine also tried to work with the same couple, but it wasn't a good fit. I had an exquisite experience that significantly helped my life, but my friend felt misunderstood and disliked it. She didn't feel the safety you need if you're going to pursue deep healing.

This brings up an important point: you've got to find the *right* therapist for you. Before you commit to a counselor, do your research into their training and specialties. Get recommended names from friends or trusted mentors. Interview the therapists before you commit to meeting regularly. Get a sense of how they would relate to you. Make sure you feel supported, safe, and confident in their abilities to help you; if you do, that's when you commit to going deep. If you are also in need of medication while you pursue healing, you need to take these same concepts and apply them to your search for a psychiatrist who can prescribe medication.

RED FLAGS

Abused people tend to gravitate towards people who are abusers, as I did for much of my life. Because of that, you have to be extremely careful that you don't choose a therapist who might take advantage of you. If you feel disrespected by a therapist, that's a red flag. If you feel like they're not hearing you or listening well—red flag.

Are they only talking *at* you? Do they pressure you to do things you're uncomfortable with? Do they break professional boundaries? Those are all red flags. If you run into any one of those warning signs, break off your relationship with that counselor and look for a healthier context to heal.

The website http://psychcrime.org/database provides a tool where you can type in the name of a potential therapist. If they have a record of criminal behavior, the database will highlight that information. Unfortunately, their list is not complete, so it's still important for you to do as much as possible to research your therapist ahead of time.

Needed Expertise

You might find a counselor that has none of these red flags but is still the wrong fit because they're not well-trained in dealing with abuse. Maybe you love this counselor—you have a great rapport, and they make you feel safe. You might even have a prior relationship with a counselor who worked with you in another area of life, and you want to return to that trusted relationship. But listen: if the counselor doesn't have effective tools to deal with your history of abuse, I believe you're wasting your time and money.

This point is important. A therapist might be an incredible specialist in marriage counseling but not know how to deal with abuse. Just because you like or respond to the person is not enough. I sought help from a lot of professionals who are good people—but they didn't do anything to help me because they didn't understand what was needed to deal with a person with physical and sexual abuse. They were happy to *learn* how to counsel abuse survivors—but wanted to learn on my nickel. You're paying a counselor for expertise, not to train them.

Later in this chapter, I provide a list of potential interview questions you could ask a therapist in your first meeting. These questions are designed to help you determine whether or not a counselor would be the right fit.

FINDING THE RIGHT THERAPIST

So, how do you find the names of therapists to call in the first place? The internet is a great place to start. Most counselors offer bios, vision statements, and credentials on their websites. You can also reference the appendix in this book for a list of organizations that offer resources and support to abuse survivors. Many of them have local chapters with numbers you can call. If you don't know where to start, call one of these organizations and ask for referrals for therapists in your area.

Maybe you're a fifteen-year-old girl in a small town,

trapped in an abusive situation with your father. You don't know how to escape, and you know there's not likely to be a group therapy session happening near you; even if there were, you couldn't drive there. How are you supposed to find a therapist? There are emergency abuse hotlines that you can call if you're in a crisis. Those hotline operators are trained to assess your situation and can offer helpful suggestions about next steps. They may not provide a perfect solution, but they can help you determine how to best find help.

You can also join a group like ASCA and ask other abuse survivors for their referrals. Word-of-mouth recommendations might come from trusted friends and family members as well. When you get a referral, get information about why they're recommending that particular therapist. Ask questions like "How well do you know this counselor? Have you worked with them personally? What's their style of counseling? Do you know their credentials?"

I recommend collecting at least three referrals. Once you've got several names of recommended therapists, make an appointment with each of them. Either on the phone or at your first session, plan to interview them using the following questions.

INTERVIEW QUESTIONS

At your first appointment with a therapist, ask them questions so that you can determine whether or not they'd be a good fit. When they respond to the questions, pay attention to the answers, but also pay attention to their voice. Are they defensive, rude, vague, or evasive? That's a bad sign. Any of those negative qualities in tone will continue in therapy, and you don't want to work with someone who makes you feel disrespected. However, if they seem thoughtful and inquisitive, and listen well to what you're saying, that's a good sign. The potential therapist should be able to fully answer your questions and convince you that they are well-qualified to deal with abuse.

Here are some of the questions you may want to ask, along with some follow-up notes about the kinds of answers you're looking for. Some of the research into a counselor's credentials and education can be done ahead of time, via Google or their website.

- *How long have you been practicing?*

    You might feel more comfortable working with someone who has been practicing for a long time, or this might not matter to you. Either way, it's important to know the depth of experience this person has.

- *What are your areas of specialty, and how did you become specialized in those areas?*

    Ideally, the prospective counselor should have extensive experience working with people who have experienced child abuse.

- *What is your theoretical basis for therapy? Why do you think this theory is effective?*[1]

    There are many different kinds of therapy that can be effective for healing sexual trauma. You don't need to look for a specific kind of theoretical basis, since many can work. However, the therapist should be *consistent* in applying this theory, and you should feel convinced from the start that it will be effective for your healing.[2]

- *What are your educational and training credentials? Where did you do your internship, and how long was it?*

    The prospective counselor should have a master's in either community counseling or marriage and family counseling from an accredited university (CACREP and CORE are the accrediting bodies; look for their affiliation). In addition to

---

1 First three interview questions from: Bobbi Parish, "Five Questions to Ask a Potential Therapist," Psych Central, March 23, 2015, https://blogs.psychcentral.com/sex-abuse/2015/03/five-questions-to-ask-a-potential-therapist/.

2 "Sexual Abuse Counselor," Psychology Careers, accessed October 11, 2018, https://www.psychology-careers.com/sexual-abuse-counselor/.

at least sixty credit hours, these degrees should have also required six hundred to nine hundred internship practicum hours with clients. It's also helpful if the therapist has a bachelor's degree in psychology or social work, although this may not be a requirement for you.[3] They should also be licensed by the state for private practice.

- *What training and/or classes have you taken about healing from sexual abuse?*

There is no special certification for a sexual abuse counselor, but all accredited master of counseling programs offer educational electives in the area of abuse and trauma.[4] Ideally, your prospective therapist will be able to mention several classes or trainings that relate specifically to abuse.

- *Do you have experience working with abuse survivors? What areas of abuse have you counseled people through?*

Make sure you work with a therapist who has extensive experience working with abuse survivors, ideally in the area you experienced abuse.

- *How often do you typically see clients? (More than once per week?) How long does your process usually take*

---

[3] Ibid.

[4] Ibid.

before a client moves on from counseling? What is your fee schedule?

These are practical questions to help you determine whether or not you'll be able to afford this counselor. If a therapist wants to meet three times a week, charges $140 a session, and expects to counsel you for several years, that could be a red flag that you're being taken advantage of. A typical counseling arrangement would be a session once a week (unless the situation is acute, in which case you'd meet more often), with a clear end goal in mind.

Pay attention to how you feel during the session. Was it encouraging? Do you feel confident about moving forward? Or are you still questioning whether or not this therapist is going to be a good fit? If you're still questioning, you should probably keep looking. You've got to feel the conversation is an honest dialogue, where they're seriously interested in the questions you're asking.

It might be hard to evaluate how you feel about a therapist; abuse survivors are not always great at listening to their intuition. Especially if someone else is pressuring you to see a certain therapist, it might be hard for you to listen to your own gut. Remember that *you* need to feel comfortable and safe with this therapist. If it's not a good fit for *you*, then it's not a good fit, period.

Trust yourself and your instincts. If a potential therapist doesn't feel right, question why. Is it because the counselor is asking questions about certain areas that are terrifying, or is it because the approach that is being taken just doesn't feel good to you? Abuse counseling *will* be scary because you're getting into incredibly painful memories. But you should still feel safe with your counselor and confident in their ability to lead you. They should respect when you can't go any further, and you should see progress in your healing.

If you don't feel like your own instincts at reading people are solid, I recommend bringing along a trusted friend or family member to your first session. Make sure this person won't pressure you to go with the therapist or not; their main goal should be to help you identify any potential red flags. The book *Allies in Healing*, by Laura Davis, offers many helpful thoughts about ways your spouse or loved ones can support you during your healing, including their role as you pursue counseling.

THE RIGHT FIT

After getting all of your questions answered in an initial session, it's time to think about fit. You could have two equally competent therapists, one you're comfortable working with and one you're not. Choose the one you're comfortable with. If it's a good fit, you're more likely to take on the challenges of healing.

In a good therapy setting, you will feel confident that you're being helped. You'll feel respected, listened to, and acknowledged. You'll be encouraged to participate in your healing and maybe even take charge of it. You'll also know from the research you did ahead of time that the therapist you're working with is well-educated, credentialed, and professionally respected.

You will feel trust with this counselor. Still, consider the old saying Ronald Reagan used to quote: "Trust, but verify." If you choose a professional and start getting into it, monitor it as you're going along. Ask yourself if it's working for you. In a good therapeutic setting, it will be—and you'll know it.

THE BEST TIME TO START THERAPY

Begin therapy as soon as possible after the abuse has occurred—the sooner, the better. I know of two children who were abused, and the family initially wanted to deal with it privately. After a required reporter sounded the alarm, the abuser was investigated and eventually arrested. Most importantly, the children got into counseling immediately, and they've been able to bounce back well from their trauma.

In order to survive, an abused person buries the pain; the longer they go before getting help, the deeper they bury.

Remember the Brené Brown quote "You can't selectively numb emotion. When you numb the dark, you numb the joy." The longer a person has spent burying their pain, the more difficult it is to return to a healthy lifestyle and restore their healthy well-being. Getting therapy as soon as possible is best.

Most of the time, when a child is hurt, they receive help immediately. When a kid falls off his bike and scrapes his knee, a loving caregiver rushes in to console him. If a child is dangerously ill, the nurturing caregiver tends to her. But in the situation of abuse, victims are so often made to feel abandoned. Especially if the abuser is supposed to be a loving caregiver, a child may not know where to turn and may feel entirely alone.

These damaged children are in danger of living damaged lives if they don't get help immediately. Hurting adolescents and young adults may resort to self-mutilation, alcohol, drugs, or sexual promiscuity, or they might become pedophiles, exhibitionists, or criminals. If you were abused, don't wait another day before seeking out help. If you know a child that's been abused, do everything you can to get them help. The faster an abused person can receive professional help, the faster and better the recovery.

In my case and perhaps in yours, decades might have

already passed since your experience of abuse. My life would have been significantly different if I hadn't waited forty years before getting help. However, there is hope! I stumbled along until I found the help I needed from people who showed me I had to look within. Healing can come to *everyone*.

THE KEY IS GETTING STARTED

Whether you choose to pursue therapy in a group setting, with a private therapist, or with both—what's most important is that you *start*. Get help. If you've never pursued healing in a supportive, safe environment, you'll find it to be incredibly powerful. If you add other healthy practices, like writing and meditation, the healing will progress even faster.

The gold standard for a therapist is one who's highly qualified, accredited, comes highly recommended, and has experience with abuse survivors. Interview them and ensure it's a good fit. Make sure you find a healing environment where you'll be shown empathy, listened to, and given the support you need to heal.

But most of all, make sure you *start*.

CHAPTER EIGHT

Fighting the Cycle of Child Abuse

Most of this book has talked about personal healing—but what about the healing of our world? There are still millions of children abused every day; those children will grow up suffering from the inner wounds of abuse and may go on to become abusers themselves. How do we fight this terrible ongoing cycle? It's worth taking a close look at what can be done and what's being done already to protect our country's most vulnerable citizens.

I've worked hard to gather the research in this chapter, and I've done my best to get it right. However, I want to acknowledge that I'm not an expert in this field, and it's possible some of the material I found is dated. Still, it was important to me to look at how abuse is being addressed on a wider scale. Abuse is so often kept hidden, and that extends to our society at large—we don't want to talk about it, and we don't want to deal with it. But if we ever hope to make a dent in the instances of abuse that occur every day, we need to take a close look at what's being done in our country to address it and think about ways we can improve.

PROGRESS IS BEING MADE

The #MeToo movement signals an increasing ability to bring the issues of abuse into the open. We are at a point in history where there's more freedom than ever before to share stories of being abused and bring abusers to justice. That's a huge step forward.

However, this new freedom doesn't seem to have impacted male victims of abuse. Although statistics show that many instances of abuse occur against men, that's discussed far less openly than abuse committed against women. This could indicate the tremendous courage women have shown in sharing their stories; it could also indicate a stigma against male victims that causes them to continue to feel great shame over sharing their stories openly.

In either case, the #MeToo movement is without question

an enormous victory over the secrecy that's surrounded this issue in the past. Critical mass is now working in our favor, for the first time in history. When more abuse survivors speak up, more abused people follow suit. There is less hesitation about pursuing healing. Critically, there is *less shame*. More people are out there conveying the message "You did nothing wrong." We're seeing a movement build towards healing, justice, and reclaimed power.

BETTER TRAINING

Thanks to better training, more people are now equipped to recognize signs of abuse and report it. Take the situation of a child who's brought to a doctor and a caregiver explains her bruises by saying, "She fell down the stairs." More so than in past generations, doctors are prepared to look closely at those bruises and bring in a professional to talk to the child. Increasingly, people are alert to the signs of abuse and prepared to speak up.

MORE AWARENESS

Awareness about abuse is increasing, inch by inch. The topic can now be discussed in many schools. As with issues like suicide, bullying, or mental health, many schools are now recognizing that it's in their students' best interest to address a tough issue head-on. The topic shows up more on social media and is moving into the shared conversation of our world. All of this increased awareness is good. It means less secrecy, less silence, less judgment.

LEGAL CHANGES

Legal landscapes have also changed. More people like teachers, social workers, medical workers, and others are now required by law to report abuse if they find out about it. There are more legal protections being extended to children and higher consequences for mandatory reporters if they fail to report. In Colorado, for instance, a parent can lose their custody rights if they fail to report child abuse.[1]

BETTER TECHNIQUES FOR INTERVIEWING CHILD VICTIMS

Let's say you have a child that's been abused, and someone alerts the authorities. The police show up, call social services, and sit down with the child to record their report of what happened. That first report is critical. That's the report that a prosecutor will use to try to get the accused abuser indicted—so if that first report is done badly, the case is doomed from the start. If it's done well, there's a

---

[1] Kristina Otterstrom, "Child Abuse & Child Custody," Lawyers.com, April 9, 2015, https://www.lawyers.com/legal-info/family-law/child-custody/child-abuse-and-child-custody.html.

much better chance of bringing that perpetrator to justice, or at least having them complete required therapy.

The problem is, children are hard to get good reports from. Many young children don't have the words they need to communicate clearly what happened, and they can be easily confused by leading questions from interviewers. Children may tell false stories around the subject of abuse because they feel afraid or feel pressure from abusers or family members. Maybe they get positive affirmation from interviewers and say whatever they think the interviewers want to hear. They may even feel confusion between what's real and what's imagined.

Unfortunately, because of how challenging it's been to get a reliable testimony from an abused child, many courts haven't been able to accept the testimony as evidence.[2] One famous case from 1990, the McMartin Preschool case, involved hundreds of children accusing their daycare providers of molesting them. Some children claimed the adult providers had also forced them to go on plane rides, drink blood, and watch animals be mutilated.[3] Although prosecutors claimed the children's testimonies were collected in a legitimate way, the defense was

---

2 William Claiborne, "No Healing in Wenatchee," *Washington Post*, June 14, 1996, https://www.washingtonpost.com/archive/politics/1996/06/14/no-healing-in-wenatchee/8afb3d3d-3977-48c7-8caf-b106aba4a08d/?noredirect=on&utm_term=.e4b1cd25a739.

3 David Shaw, "Where Was Skepticism in Media?" *LA Times*, January 19, 1990.

able to cast doubt on the children's reports because of interviewers' leading questions. As a result, no convictions were made, and likely criminals were allowed to go free.[4] However, because of some of these cases, the justice system has worked to reform the process of interviewing children. A science has been developed to help first responders interview children effectively, called forensic interviewing; this method is highly professional and carefully crafted.[5] I won't go into the specifics of the best practice recommendations for forensic interviewing because, number one, I'm not an expert in this field, and number two, they're continually being updated as new research is published. However, I've cited an excellent guide in the footnotes below, from the US Office of Juvenile Justice and Delinquency Prevention (see "Child Forensic Interviewing: Best Practices").

When children are properly interviewed, and their claims are carefully explored without leading questions, their testimonies are considered to be much stronger evidence. As a result, there have been more successful prosecutions of abusers—that's an amazing step forward.[6]

---

[4] Nancy E. Walker, "Forensic Interviews of Children: The Components of Scientific Validity and Legal Admissibility," *Law and Contemporary Problems* 65, no. 1 (Winter 2002): 149–178.

[5] Chris Newlin et al., "Child Forensic Interviewing: Best Practices," U.S. Department of Justice. Office of Juvenile Justice and Delinquency Prevention (2015), Ojjdp.gov.

[6] Irit Hershkowitz, Michael E. Lamb, and Carmit Katz, "Allegation Rates in Forensic Child Abuse Investigations: Comparing the Revised and Standard NICHD Protocols," *Psychology, Public Policy, and Law* 20, no. 3 (August 2014): 336–344, http://psycnet.apa.org/doiLanding?doi=10.1037/a0037391.

Still, there's progress yet to be made. Right now, many education programs—both undergraduate and graduate—don't teach students how to deal with instances of abuse beyond mandated reporting. If you're a hospital worker, teacher, pharmacist, childcare provider, or in any number of other professions, you are required by law to report instances of neglect or harm. Because of their education, many people "get that," and they're doing that, which is a good thing.

However, many of the people going into mandated reporting professions aren't prepared to effectively interview children using proper forensic interviewing techniques; they may not even know a child *should* be interviewed using forensic interviewing techniques. If a child comes to a trusted teacher and tells her she's being abused, that teacher needs to know how to handle that conversation. As we've discussed, well-meaning adults can easily jeopardize a child's account of what happened if they ask leading questions. Undergraduate and graduate programs need to teach students the proper forensic interviewing techniques, along with whom to have at that interview and how to protect the child during questioning.

Conducting effective interviews is a particular area that should be required learning for all mandatory reporters. If more people are educated in forensic interviewing, more reports of abuse will hold up better in court. That means more kids will be protected, and more perpetrators will be put in jail, or, if appropriate, required to complete mandatory therapy.

CHALLENGES WITH FIGHTING THE CYCLE OF ABUSE

Unfortunately, there are still many obstacles to ending abuse. Victor Vieth, attorney and director of the American Prosecutors Research Institute's National Center for Prosecution of Child Abuse, estimated that it will take at least 120 years before we can end child abuse—in other words, at least three generations.[7] That 120-year "timer" would start once the powers that be in our country decide to aggressively fight child abuse through changing laws and education. Until those big moves are made, the timer remains stopped, and future generations are still at risk for continuing the cycle of abuse.

I've tried to identify some of the areas holding back positive change and have compiled ideas for "next steps" in each of these areas. As the previous chapters of this book prove, abuse is not simple! My own story of recovering from abuse took decades, required support from many different people, and went through different stages; that's what any societal healing is going to look like too.

---

[7] Victor I. Vieth, "Unto the Third Generation," *Journal of Aggression, Maltreatment, and Trauma* 12, no. 3 (October 11, 2008): 5–54, doi: https://doi.org/10.1300/J146v12n03_02.

Perhaps, though, if we get experts involved, the societal changes need not take as long! The effects of abuse are far-reaching, on a personal level and systemic level. So, even though I've identified ideas for next steps, I want to acknowledge that my suggestions are basic. In order for them to be implemented well, experts in the field would need to take up the charge and implement them in a way that helps address all the complexities. But if they're going to take up a charge, someone has to make the charge in the first place, right? So—as a starting place—I'm giving it a try.

OVERWHELMED CASEWORKERS

In Victor Vieth's article "Unto the Third Generation," he quotes reporter Anna Quindlen, who describes the extreme odds facing social workers: "Their training is inadequate, and the number of workers is too small for the number of families in trouble. Some of the cases would require a battalion of cops, doctors, and social workers to handle; instead, there are two kids fresh out of college with good intentions and a handful of forms."[8] Vieth puts most of the blame for this stress on inadequate education. Social work programs, he claims, teach about statistics and trends, but there isn't enough practical training. One social worker mentioned that, although

---

8   Anna Quindlen, "Foreword," in *Turning Stones: My Days and Nights with Children at Risk* by Marc Parent (New York: Ballantine, 1998).

he'd had "two weeks of solemn discussion on child protective issues, [there was] little on getting a drug dealer to let you into an abandoned building or talking a restless police officer into sticking around until you get through with a case and back into your car."[9]

In Vieth's same article, he describes the enormous number of child abuse reports that are made—but then are *ignored*.[10] There simply aren't enough Child Protective Services workers to address each report of abuse that comes in. The workers that are there are exhausted, overwhelmed, underpaid, beyond maximum capacity, and often burned out; the turnover in social work is huge. These social workers are an abused child's best hope for an advocate, but what happens if they simply don't have the time for that next child?

Where to Go Next: Improved and Continued Education

Because social workers aren't adequately trained about the challenges they'll confront, it takes them a long time to effectively get up to speed. Only when their knowledge, familiarity with the challenges, and resources all align are they able to make a real difference—but by the time

---

9   Marc Parent, *Turning Stones: My Days and Nights with Children at Risk* (New York: Ballantine, 1998).

10 Victor I. Vieth, "Unto the Third Generation," *Journal of Aggression, Maltreatment, and Trauma* 12, no. 3 (October 11, 2008): 5–54, doi: https://doi.org/10.1300/J146v12n03_02.

that happens, half of them quit. They're fighting an uphill battle, and they get burned out. If programs make sure social workers have all those factors aligned when they *enter* the field, they could make a powerful difference with less burnout.

Continued education is also needed to update social workers, police, attorneys, and other relevant workers on new best practices. There are constant new findings about what people are doing out there, what's working, and what's not working. It's easy to get set in a familiar approach because "that's how it's always been done." Continued education can help break that, and even help keep workers enthusiastic about what they're doing. Better training means better protection of children, which is energizing for all child advocates.

Other factors would obviously make a huge difference in the level of social worker turnover, such as better pay, more emotional support, larger staff, and so on. However, targeting improvements at the education level is a good place to start.

UNHEALTHY POWER DYNAMICS

For most of history, men have controlled the family; women and children were viewed as property. This attitude meant that if a man felt like beating his child, he beat her or him; if he felt like abusing his wife, he did. Although attitudes have hugely changed about men and women's roles in the last century, there's still an underlying attitude among some men that they have the right to dominate. That can easily translate into abuse.

The #MeToo movement has pointed out all the areas where men have abused power for their own sexual pleasure. In Hollywood, in politics, on college campuses, even in the church, people were abused by powerful men and then pressured to keep their stories silent. Not only that, the systems around the abusers have protected them. Up until recently, male college students rarely ever got prosecuted for raping a girl. Look at Penn State, where the assistant coach was having sex with young athletes, and it was known, but he wasn't fired.[11] Hollywood producer Harvey Weinstein's people paid women off or threatened their careers to keep them quiet.[12] The Catholic Church lobbied for rules that would shorten the statute of limitations and moved abusive priests around to different parishes.[13] You've got systemic problems protecting the abusers.

---

[11] CNN Library, "Penn State Scandal Fast Facts," CNN, last modified March 28, 2018, https://www.cnn.com/2013/10/28/us/penn-state-scandal-fast-facts/index.html.

[12] Jodi Kantor and Megan Twohey, "Harvey Weinstein Paid Off Sexual Harassment Accusers for Decades," *New York Times*, October 05, 2017, https://www.nytimes.com/2017/10/05/us/harvey-weinstein-harassment-allegations.html.

[13] George Joseph, "US Catholic Church Has Spent Millions Fighting Clergy Sex Abuse Accountability," *Guardian*, May 12, 2016, https://www.theguardian.com/us-news/2016/may/12/catholic-church-fights-clergy-child-sex-abuse-measures.

Men are not the only abusers; many instances of child sexual abuse are perpetrated by women. This abuse couldn't be blamed on misogyny in our culture (misogyny is defined as the hatred of women), but there are shared themes of dominating, abusing power, and taking advantage of the vulnerable. For instance, women are more likely to abuse younger children. Also, abuse from women often falls into the "teacher/student" category, when an older woman preys on a younger male.[14] One study found that "In juvenile corrections facilities, female staff are...a much more significant threat than male staff; more than nine in ten juveniles who reported staff sexual victimization were abused by a woman."[15] Whether men or women are carrying out the abuse, it's the vulnerable who are made victims.

We need a collective agreement that this is not okay. Perpetrators of abuse—no matter what kind of power they have in society—should not be allowed to get away with abuse. These unhealthy attitudes about power need to be rooted out of our culture.

---

14   Xanthe Mallett, "Women Also Sexually Abuse Children, but Their Reasons Often Differ from Men's," *The Conversation*, February 19, 2017, http://theconversation.com/women-also-sexually-abuse-children-but-their-reasons-often-differ-from-mens-72572.

15   Lara Stemple and Ilan H. Meyer, "Sexual Victimization by Women Is More Common Than Previously Known," *Scientific American*, October 10, 2017, https://www.scientificamerican.com/article/sexual-victimization-by-women-is-more-common-than-previously-known/.

Where to Go Next: Grassroots Education

We can hope and push for change to come from the top, but—given the track record of leaders like the ones I just mentioned—we'd better expect to work for that change from the bottom up. We need to "uproot" by planting new roots! That grassroots change will begin with *educating* more people and building their awareness about the unique challenges of child abuse. The general public must be educated through organizations like Resilient People. That responsibility also falls on faith communities, schools, colleges, universities, and the political system.

The area of education is obviously connected to schools and politics—but why should faith communities get involved? Regardless of what you might think of organized religion, faith communities still wield a lot of power. People look to them for guidance and direction. They have the ability to make people care deeply about certain issues, especially those in line with their holy texts. All prophets spoke about helping children; Jesus said, "Let the little children come unto me."[16] Helping victims of abuse is in line with many churches' missions to fight oppression and help the needy. An often-overlooked way that churches can help end child abuse is through *educating* their parishioners about the issue. There's an enormous educational platform available in church

---
16 Luke 18:16, New International Version.

bodies, and they can help make a real impact in raising awareness.

Particularly given the Catholic Church's terrible number of sexual abuse scandals, they should consider it a duty and obligation to take the lead on these educational efforts. In an act of repentance, they should take deliberate steps to not just remove predatory priests, but to actively work towards building awareness about abuse and promoting healing. The Catholic leaders were guilty in many parishes of committing abuse; now, they should work at fighting abuse. They kept secrets; now, they should be the first to shed light. Perhaps, through efforts like this, they might be able to once again symbolize redemption, rather than scandal.

NO POWERFUL ADVOCATES FOR CHILDREN

The #MeToo movement has caused an incredible shift in our culture towards holding perpetrators accountable for abuse. However, it also highlights a unique problem facing the effort to end child abuse. The #MeToo movement was given momentum when some powerful women actors in Hollywood stepped forward, risked their careers, and spoke up about times they were abused. As a result, many other women followed suit, and now these men in charge are being toppled. If you're powerful, you have a voice—and you can create positive change.

The problem is, abused children have no voice; they have no power. What famed child actor is going to step forward with his story of abuse and create a sea change like the #MeToo movement? Children are scared, vulnerable, and terrified to speak up. That means adults have to advocate for them. *We* have to speak up for them because children have no voice of their own. And what's more, this effort is going to require a constant beating of the drum, getting people to hear this.

Where to Go Next: More Vocal Advocacy and Funding

If we're going to create societal change, more adult survivors need to speak up and be advocates for the children. There are hundreds of small organizations like Resilient People; I think there are far more people involved than we even realize. If all the splinter groups formed a massive national unit, the power to influence would grow exponentially. There needs to be vocal advocacy, local chapters, and an educational arm focused on raising greater awareness.

As a national organization, we would endeavor to get a lot of media. People should feel the tension of child abuse; they need to be increasingly aware of the problem. We also need to publicize and drill down the fact that these children did nothing wrong. They were truly victims of somebody who had power over them. The child might have been manipulated through a close relationship with the perpetrator or may have been overcome by the power of physical force; regardless, they were abused by someone who had power over them. In so many instances, the abuser took it further by leading the child to believe it was their fault. We need to get the message out that victims of abuse do not need to feel shame.

There also needs to be money. Although it shouldn't be, money is a huge part of this. If you're able to get your message in front of Congress, you'd better have some money in your back pocket. Moral issues on their own have not gotten much traction in recent decades. However, the large, well-funded organizations—like the NRA or Big Pharma—get heard.

Money also needs to be channeled towards better compensation of workers in the field and continued education. Put bluntly, our society currently does not value children enough to pour money into their welfare. Just think about the typical condition of a school bus—there are no seat belts and few rivets, and the seats are hard and rubbery—but the attitude is that they're "good enough" for kids. Stronger advocacy groups could help push for better funding to be channeled into the care of children. The funding issue is another reason why smaller organizations would accomplish more if they banded together.

Like the old saying goes, there's strength in numbers. Powerful men and powerful women need to give abused children a voice.

COMPLEX REASONS FOR DENIAL OR SECRECY

I've had several experiences recently where I was talking to friends of mine about this book. I said to some of them, "Guys, I want to tell you about what I'm working on." I gave them each a Resilient People card. I never heard back from one of them. People don't want to acknowledge the severity of the problem and that it's most likely occurring in their own neighborhood; it could even be their neighbor. It's a painful subject, especially if it's hidden somewhere in somebody's life. However, until there's more widespread acknowledgment that children are experiencing terrible violence every day—the change is not going to come.

Unfortunately, even in the areas where people are painfully aware that abuse is happening, there may still be denial. One of the biggest areas of secrecy is when abuse occurs within the family. Families don't want to discuss the fact that abuse might be happening in their home. There's pressure on children to stay silent because chaos can ensue when a report is made; the parents might get arrested, and children could end up in the social services network, away from their family. Also, children often still feel loyalty to their families, and fear what might happen to them if they speak up. In the best-case scenario, an abused child speaks up, a trusted adult reports it, and social services are able to work with the family to create a safer environment. However, that optimal scenario requires the participation and support of the entire family, which often doesn't happen. It's rarely that neat or that simple.

One of the biggest factors why more abuse victims don't speak up—as I can personally testify—is that it's *complicated*. People choose not to report because of highly personal reasons. They often have intimate relationships with the abuser, like I did. Some people may have reported in the past and, for whatever reason, the outcome was not what they'd hoped for. Some people fear they won't be believed or that they might even be blamed. There's also a feeling of distrust of the police in some communities.

There's any number of reasons to ignore this problem, deny it's happening, or keep quiet while enduring the pain. These are complex issues, and there's no easy way to address any of them. But perhaps there's a place to start.

Where to Go Next: Community Leaders

If more survivors of abuse are going to share their stories, they need to be surrounded by more safe people. It's up to community leaders to be those safe people and mentor others in being those safe people too. Any reader of this book is likely someone who cares deeply about ending child abuse. You might be an incredible candidate for a community leader in creating positive change.

If you're a teacher, you might take it upon yourself to read the latest findings and trends about how to address abuse from an educational context. You could present those findings at staff meetings or make sure you get the articles to the school counselors. You'll also be better equipped to identify a concerning situation with a student and make a report if need be. If you work in law enforcement, you can advocate for new trainings for other members of your department. If you're in a faith community, ask for Sunday school classes about ways the church can help victims of abuse. Write letters to your congresspeople and show up to town meetings. Run for office!

Community leaders can make a powerful difference because they know the needs of their local area. Teachers know each child in their classroom. Patrol officers know the families who repeatedly call with reports of domestic abuse. Social workers know the specific needs of different neighborhoods. Community leaders also know the trends in communication and culture, so they can tailor information for their specific community. A policeman from a small town in the South is going to have a different approach to raising awareness about abuse than a cop in New York City—and that's a good thing.

If you believe strongly in this issue, you can find a way to make your voice heard. Although many workers in the careers just mentioned are overloaded already, there's a unique calling for people who know firsthand the pain of abuse. Perhaps this calling is yours!

OUR MISSION

Before you take up this charge, though, I'm going to tell you to heal yourself first. You must learn on the deepest level that you did absolutely nothing wrong as a child. Second, embrace the truth that you can lead a productive, beautiful life. Despite all that you've experienced as a result of sexual abuse, and despite the cloak of shame you may have worn for most of your life, you can heal. Before trying to heal others, heal yourself first.

The power that abuse carries from childhood into adulthood is strong; it impacts the way we think and interrupts us at every turn. It interrupts our social engagements, our friendships, our relationships, our marriages, our businesses. Negative emotions leak out and ruin all the good things. That's why we have to personally heal before we're any good in a service capacity.

Sometimes people turn to service as a crutch. Rather than face the pain and suffering of their reality, they distract themselves by trying to help others. It becomes an excuse to not do their own hard work of healing. But you *need* to do that healing. You need to get clarity about what really works for you and what doesn't. What is acceptable? What is unacceptable? What feels good for your soul? When you come to that clarity, you can take a stand for what you believe in, and you can avoid what's toxic.

A bad therapist can hurt people more than help them. Similarly, if you're still damaged while you're trying to help someone, you can actually mess them up more. Something they say might trigger you, then suddenly you're breaking down, and the person you're supposed to be helping is trying to help you. While you're still working through your own healing, you're in danger of transferring your own pain to someone else. You don't yet have the knowledge or the wisdom to truly be of help to others.

Once you've walked your own healing path, you're going to be able to help someone from a knowledgeable standpoint. You know the journey, you know the side roads, you know the hang-ups, and you know what it's going to take to get there. However, when you've healed, you have a better chance of being successful in your own life and truly helping other people. Do we ever get there, 100 percent? I'm still not 100 percent, but I've gotten to a place where the shame has drained out of my body. I've exchanged darkness for light and faith in a higher power. I can tell my story to others without breaking down, and I can see things more objectively now.

You can break through your own shame. When you break through all the darkness you've carried inside you, you can use the power you've regained for good. You will have new power within your consciousness and new power from regaining the truth of who you are. With that newfound strength and energy, join an organization. Work in your local community. Build this voice up until the crescendo is so powerful and so loud, Congress can't ignore it. Make the voice loud enough that the money sources can't ignore it. Help rescue future children from lives shattered by abuse.

But that can't be your first goal. Your main hope can be found in the truth that *you* can heal. Know the truth about yourself: you did nothing wrong. Don't wait for society to change; society will not change you personally. Until you deal with the depths of your own being to excavate and transmute your shame—your deep grief—into light and joy, you'll still be locked in a battle. Yes, there's a risk in going forward and dealing with it; there's also a risk in *not* dealing with it. If you don't deal with it, you'll stay in the same old sewer and maybe sink deeper. If you deal with it, your life will get better. You can live a joyful and beautiful life.

So first: rescue you.

Conclusion

I sat alone in my home office in Durango, looking down at the letter in my hands. I stared at the words detailing the total violation he'd committed. I read over accusations about the pornographic videos, and how they'd destroyed my understanding of how to truly love a woman. I read words describing destroyed trust and perverted love. I read the letter and reread the letter. Finally, I dialed his number.

I was nervous. How could I not be? But I was also focused and determined.

The phone rang. A voice picked up on the other end of the line. "Hello?" It was an old man's voice, but I still recognized it immediately. That voice had haunted me for most of my life.

It was the voice of Bob.

For months leading up to this moment, I'd been meeting with my therapist, Dr. Rosana Scearce; she's a top psychologist in Houston who works with abuse survivors. She had heard me process the abuse from Bob and my work on forgiving him. I had a confused understanding of forgiveness, though. I thought if I was going to forgive someone, I had to like them again; I had to invite them back into my life. In an effort to do that with Bob, I found myself making excuses for him. Rosana heard me say at times, "Oh, he loved me. He did actually love me."

She pushed back on that. "Rick, he didn't love you. He sexually abused you. He knew he was going to abuse you from the beginning—he just had to bide his time in order to build up enough trust."

There were two sides of my memories of Bob. I was clear on the fact that Bob was a pedophile, but there was another part of me that remembered feeling unloved as a child and finding that desperately-wanted attention from him. On those vacations in the Catskills, my father always worked. He never came out swimming or playing with us. Then, I have these memories of Bob taking me for rides in his police car and going swimming with me and my friends—it was exhilarating. But it was also perverted.

He took the love I'd developed for him and used it for his own sexual pleasure.

Rosana could see that confusion. She knew that before I could make any progress in healing from abuse, I needed to recognize the truth about what he did to me: he wasn't a loving adult figure in my life. He was a pedophile. He was a predator.

One day she asked, "Have you ever confronted Bob?" I shrugged and told her no. "Why not?" she asked.

"Well," I said, "I've done a lot of forgiveness work. I figured I was going to let it go."

She pushed back on that. "I want you to think about that. This is a guy who pretended to love you and used that to sexually abuse you."

I began to realize I'd been giving Bob a pass, and it made me angry. I spoke more with Rosana about it and decided I wanted to confront him. She instructed me to keep notes over the next week and write down every negative thing I could remember about Bob. "None of the good stuff," she ordered me. "Nothing about the ride in the police car or cleaning the gun. I want you to think about what he *did*." I followed her instructions. Over the next week, I filled up a shoebox with note cards, each one with a detail about how he'd harmed me.

When I spoke to Rosana again, I asked, "What now?" She instructed me to bury the box somewhere on my property. I got a shovel out of my garage and went into the field. I tried breaking the soil, but it was December and the ground was frozen solid. That stumped me, temporarily. Where was I going to find a hole in December? How was I going to bury Bob? Then I came up with a brilliant idea.

I found a porta potty. I went in, dumped the box down the hole, and then sat on the seat. I proceeded to do my business. I thought, "How wonderful. I'm finally shitting on this guy. And the whole town of Durango is going to shit on him, too, when this winds up in the sewer treatment plant!" Rosana almost died laughing when I told her that.

Then I wrote the letter. I called my brother and asked if Bob was still alive. He confirmed Bob was still around and managed to get me his phone number. He asked, "Why do you want it?"

I said, "I've got a few things to say to him." The next day I called.

Bob answered the phone. I said, "Bob, this is Freddy Huttner."

He sounded delighted. "Freddy! Freddy, I'm so happy to hear from you. This is wonderful. It's been so long since I've seen you."

I said, "Bob, I've got some things to say."

I read the letter. I told him that the perverted form of love he used to sexually abuse me had seriously harmed my life. I said, "I know who you are. You're a sexual predator, you're a pervert, and you're a disgrace." He tried to interrupt me at that point, but I got louder and wouldn't stop. I was not about to let him control our interaction. I ended with, "Bob, I hope you live the rest of your life in hell." Then I hung up.

My letter didn't sound forgiving, and it wasn't meant to be forgiving. I was confronting a charismatic pedophile who abused multiple children while wearing a badge. I wanted him to experience some of the hell he had created for other people. That's probably not a nice thing, but this wasn't about being nice. This was about making a statement, once and for all, that I knew the truth of who he was and what he'd done.

The second I hung up the phone, I felt like a weight had been lifted from my soul and my consciousness. I didn't expect that. It was beautiful—I felt wonderful! I texted Rosana, and I said, "I did it! I did it! I did it!" I called my mentor from ManKind Project, and I told my brother. After decades of feeling beaten down by my abuser, it felt like I'd finally fought a battle for Little Freddy and won. It freed the child within me.

Was justice served? No: justice would have been much more severe. But I was able to take my power back. I was able to control the situation—something I was never able to do as a thirteen-year-old boy. The experience brought a conclusion to the long shadow Bob had cast over my life. Now, Bob is insignificant. He holds nothing over me. I'm now able to tell my story publicly, with no shame. My story of abuse has become just a story.

YOUR HEALING JOURNEY

It has been fifty years since I began my healing journey. It's taken me half a century to realize that I could heal, and I knew that I didn't want others to wait that long to experience freedom and joy. The spark inside of me, what I like to think of as a Divine Presence, urged me to begin turning my focus towards helping others. Very few adult males talk publicly about being abused. I realized I had a message for them—for all survivors of abuse.

I formed Resilient People to create a platform for that message: *You are resilient. You did nothing wrong. You can overcome all of this and take your power back.* I share my story and drive that message home at speaking engagements. People have come up to me afterwards and thanked me; they've told me my message of healing has helped improve their lives. What a gift to be able to experience helping others, after so many years of not even being able to help myself!

To those people who contact me, and to every person reading this book who has acknowledged the painful presence of abuse in their past, I say this: what you're doing is courageous and good. You're stepping on a road to take a journey of healing. You will get there! I've said it before, but I can't say it enough: you can absolutely heal. You did nothing wrong as a child. It's the caregiver's responsibility to protect the child, no matter what.

Consider finding a group where you can tell your story to empathetic listeners who will support you and not judge you. Think also about doing private work, where you can dig deep with a professional. Find the appropriate person to heal with, and don't be embarrassed to check out their record, their counseling philosophy, and their experience. Ask questions. If you sense it isn't the right fit, trust your gut and find someone else. I've included an appendix with resources in an effort to help you find some of these healthy places to heal. If you don't have any idea where to start, try me. Go to www.resilientpeople.us and send me an email or give me a call. I can help point you in the right direction.

As you pursue healing, I encourage you to allow the painful feelings to rise and let yourself feel them. Pay attention to your thinking patterns. Write out your observations. Train yourself to let the negative thoughts go and choose positive thoughts instead. Most importantly, *open yourself up to good and commit to healing*. I believe that when you do that, the Divine will support you, and you will learn to love yourself.

I will never again be ashamed about what happened to me or my desire to tell this story to help others. My hope for you is that you can one day claim this same motto. Abuse no longer needs to control us; *we* control our own destiny. Put your stake in the ground and commit to healing. I came to a point in my life where the fear of moving forward was outweighed by the pain of staying where I was. It's a risk to choose healing—but it's the best risk you'll ever take. Take your power back.

Appendix

OTHER RESOURCES

Please note: if you are in need of immediate help facing an emotional crisis that you feel is too painful to bear and are considering hurting yourself or someone else, **call 911** *or one of the following numbers:*

- The National Suicide Hotline: 1-800-273-8255
- The National Sexual Assault Hotline/RAINN: 1-800-656-4673. (When you call this number, you'll be routed to a local RAINN affiliate organization, based on the first six digits of your phone number. You'll be able to have a confidential conversation with a trained staff member and learn about what support is available.)

There is help and assistance waiting for your call. YOU ARE NOT ALONE. Reach out!

1. **Adult Survivors of Child Abuse: ASCA.** The two basic components of the ASCA program are individually reading and working the *Survivor to Thriver* manual and participating in the ASCA meetings. Meetings are the backbone of the ASCA recovery program.
2. **Abuse: Support Groups Resources / Psych Central.** Psych Central is a resource website that identifies programs and information to assist child abuse victims in gaining information on childhood sexual abuse resources.
3. **National Association of Adult Survivors of Child Abuse: NAASCA.** A national charity that deals with issues of child abuse and trauma (http://facebook.com/groups/naasca).
4. **WINGS Foundation: Adult Survivors of Childhood Sexual Abuse.** Discusses common trauma symptoms in WINGS support groups and provides help in finding the right therapist.
5. **Survivors of Incest Anonymous.** This is a twelve-step spiritual self-help group for victims of sexual abuse, ages eighteen and over, who want to recover. There are no dues or fees.
6. **Help for Adult Victims of Child Abuse: HAVOCA.** HAVOCA is run by survivors of child abuse and pro-

vides support, friendship, and advice for any adult whose life has been affected by childhood abuse. Their website includes many resources to aid in recovery. They stand by the belief that every single child abuse survivor has the ability to survive and lead a more fulfilling life.
7. **Survivors: The Enough Abuse Campaign.** Offers resources for adults who have experienced childhood sexual abuse and are seeking support.
8. **Childhelp.** Childhelp is one of the largest national nonprofit child abuse prevention and treatment organizations. They help the victims of child abuse through education, treatment, and prevention programs.

There are many organizations to choose from, and I have not been able to interview these groups firsthand; therefore, I can't personally recommend one. As I have said in the book, getting help is critical to healing, but where you get the help is also critical. Choose thoughtfully and know that, if one doesn't work for you, there are many to choose from.

BOOKS THAT YOU MAY FIND HELPFUL FOR HEALING

Allies in Healing: When the Person You Love was Sexually Abused as a Child, by Laura Davis. Quoted several times in this book, this text helps loved ones of abuse survivors know how to help in the healing process.

The Courage to Heal and *The Courage to Heal Workbook*, also by Laura Davis. This is a classic resource for women who were sexually abused as children.

Healing the Shame That Binds You, by John Bradshaw. This book focuses on "toxic shame": the feelings of hopelessness, worthlessness, and inadequacy that many adult survivors of childhood abuse carry into their adult lives.

Outgrowing the Pain: A Book for and about Adults Abused as Children, by Eliana Gil, PhD. This book helps abuse survivors identify destructive patterns in their lives and move towards healing.

Soul Survivors: A New Beginning for Adults Abused as Children, by J. Patrick Gannon, PhD. This recovery guide for abuse survivors incorporates ASCA's twenty-one steps and is research-based throughout.

Victims No Longer: Men Recovering from Incest and Other Sexual Child Abuse, by Michael Lew. Childhood sexual abuse happens to boys as well as girls, and this excellent book focuses on the experience of men who were sexually abused as children.

Acknowledgments

Ann Huttner: My wife has supported me through the healing process, which was not always easy. Ann reads everything I write and assists me in making my work better. She is my friend, she is my partner, and she is a blessing in my life and the lives of our children.

Our children: Maury, Mesia, Chris, and Aaron. Special thanks to Mesia for being a constant support.

Chance Taureau: One of my senior leaders in ManKind Project, Chance has helped guide me and other men towards living lives of greater purpose and integrity. Along with his leadership in ManKind Project, Chance is a director of Resilient People. He was, and is, an invaluable source of guidance, love, and support in the process of writing this book. We meet every Wednesday, with few exceptions. Chance, you are a blessing to me and many others.

Matt Kelly: Along with Chance, Matt has been my senior leader in ManKind Project. His leadership has guided men to release their dark and controlling shadows and helped me reveal the light and truth of my own being.

Jesse Marion: I'm thankful to Jesse for his incredible support, both personally and financially. He has generously supported this book and Resilient People. His friendship is a beautiful gift in my life and many lives. He is truly a generous and loving man. I am blessed that we are in life together.

Howard Caesar: Howard has been my friend for over thirty years and is the former senior minister of Unity Church of Christianity. He's the author of *One + One Is One*, a dear friend, and a gift to me and this planet.

Jesse Jennings: Jesse is an author and the minister of Creative Life Church, a place of wisdom, love, learning, and compassion where I continued my healing. Jesse gave me my first chance to speak to his congregation, and I will always hold this in my heart.

Rosana Scearce: Dr. Scearce is an author and speaker, widely acknowledged for her work with abused children and survivors of childhood abuse. Dr. Scearce is also a director of Resilient People and has been significant in developing our workshops. She is a friend, a valuable member of the Resilient team, and a top professional in the healing of abuse.

Greta Myers and Ted Flanagan: Greta and Ted have been invaluable in guiding me through the writing of this book. Greta is elegant in demanding excellence and allows me to come away smiling.

Dick Bueltel: Dick is my best friend and pal who assisted in the original artwork and brochure for Resilient People. Most important, he's been a constant support and inspiration.

Brad Barber: Brad, along with Dick, assisted in the original artwork and design for the initial brochure.

Shirley Sandlin and Ruth "The Truth" Catalonga: These women have been great guides to the beauty of life.

Todd Youngblood, Abbi Pittman, and Drew Semel were significant in the development of the Resilient Website. Abbi took the work of Todd and Drew and created the beautiful website www.resilientpeople.us. Abbi is talented, professional, and fun to work with.

Randa Fox, founder of Not on Our Watch and ASCA

group leader in Houston, assisted in research to make this a better book. Randa is committed to ending child abuse.

Barry Hayes is my friend who helped lay out the original plan for Resilient.

John Babbs is a dear friend and love personified.

My brothers, Bob, Andy, and especially Richie Huttner.

Beulah Clay Edmonds: minister and midwife. Beulah guided me back to the love of the Divine. She has passed and will always hold a place in my heart.

Thank you to all my friends who have been there to support me in so many loving ways.

About Frederick "Rick" Huttner

I am seventy-three years of age. I am healthy, joyful, have a beautiful loving wife, four great kids, six grandkids, and four "grand dogs." Life is good. It was not always so.

As an infant, I experienced physical abuse from my mother when she experienced a serious nervous breakdown, and I experienced sexual abuse as an adolescent from a friend of our family—a man I looked up to and admired. These two experiences had a profound effect on my life, both physically and mentally. This book is about how I healed (and continue to heal) and information I believe will help adult survivors of child abuse heal.

And I promise, you can heal. You and I did nothing wrong

as children to receive the abuse perpetrated upon us, whether the abuse was neglect, psychological, physical, or sexual. We were abused mostly by people we knew, and many times by people we loved. Abuse is rarely perpetrated by a person who is not known to the abused. Think of the horror of this statement: we were hurt by people we trusted. Abuse destroys trust, subverts love, and leaves the victim cloaked in shame and mentally damaged.

This book was difficult for me to write. Much of what happened to me I buried deep into my subconscious mind because it was too painful to remember. This is normal for children that have experienced abuse. It was how I survived, and it's how many of us survive.

To free myself, I needed to free my mind from the buried emotions. This was challenging, but a necessary step in the healing process. Encouraging these painful memories to come to my conscious mind and fully experiencing them allowed me to release them and replace them with the truth of who I am: a beautiful and loving person, especially to myself.

My dream is to let adult survivors of abuse, in any of its ugly forms, know they can heal and live a joyful and productive life.

My other dream is to create an awareness in our society of

the extent of abuse and its long-term damaging effects on our children, and create a society where children have a voice and advocates to ensure they can be heard, believed, and healed.

www.ingramcontent.com/pod-product-compliance
Lightning Source LLC
LaVergne TN
LVHW041613070426
835507LV00008B/220